Dearest SUICIDE

Book 2

Sometimes,
DEATH
becomes the only option.

DEAREST SUICIDE

...sometimes DEATH becomes the only option.

Dearest
SUICIDE

BOOK 2

*Sometimes, DEATH becomes
the only option…*

Just when you thought the mystery was over,

The saga just began!

Caution:
A curse to live with;
A cause to die for.

PaGidi Expressions
The Emotionally Wired

My expressions…

a window to the thoughts of my mind;

an outcry from the pains in my heart;

a personal letter to an odd listener I wouldn't have imagined talking to.

Through each page, you'll experience…

emotional pains;

controversial facts;

multiple obsessions;

countless secrets;

undeniable truths.

By connecting with my expressions,

You will realize how deep-shit and

Crazy (read: filled with so many

Fake-lies and honest-pretenses)

This life truly is.

And how you can

Start to see yourself

For who you truly are.

In a way I wish I did…

…before I chose to die.

Personally Expressed by: Me.
Personally Written for: You

About the Book…

He happily wrote his final papers after spending six years for a 5 year course, only to realize he has seven carryover courses and an automatic extra year!

On the flip side, his relationship is hitting the rocks, as his lover is stalling on a reply after seven months. At home, he's having a hard time dealing with his father's erratic behaviors and insults, which gives him traumatic episodes and a low self-esteem as he struggles to find his place between adolescence, teen age, and adulthood.

Locked in the middle of his life, his love, and his emotions, he takes a decision no one expected of him or saw coming.

In this long-anticipated and patiently awaited sequel, PaGidi continues the tale in his usual heart-grabbing and edge-of-your-seat conversational style by switching the rail from the main point of narrative about his heroic pursuit of love in the midst of his academic woes, picking up from right where the Mystery ended by giving us livid depths to circumstances leading to tragic deaths amongst teenagers, while baring it all in a villain role by revealing straight-from-the-heart conversations about his girlfriend whom he restricted to writing only emails to him as against calls…as he begins his…second relationship?

This book carries deep secrets, collects undocumented tragedies from extensive research, uncovers hidden mysteries, and breaks down age-long myths about the subject of suicide. You are about to experience twists, turns, intrigues, suspense, anguish, tension, crises, counter plots, and epic clashes, in this story with several parts: a depressive-romantic thriller, a teenage crisis, a family rollercoaster, a self-help manual, and a real-time relationship saga, amongst other telling, engaging, scourging, and provoking tales.

Dearest Suicide will make you laugh, cry, annoyed, and perplexed; making you ask questions in dumbfounding rhetoric and at some point, leaving you to scream out loud in anger… as you critically analyze things for yourself, while gaining broader insight and view into a problem that'll make you feel like your life is in the story.

THIS ISN'T A FICTION. THIS IS REALITY!

Cover Design: Emmanuel Ojodun (www.instagram.com/emmanuelojodun)

Cover Photography: Topstar (+2348068189140)

Muse: PaGidi

Edited by: AngelGabriEl Taiwo Olawale (olawalegt@gmail.com/+2347037670976)

Proof-read by: Daniel Fakunmoju; Humphery C. Shayo; Oluwapelumi Awotedu

ISBN:

Reactions to PaGidi Expressions…

TOCHUKWU PRECIOUS EZE (DI MADWRITER) |Author of Tobé, Adaeze, Mirror; Founder, Mental Health Awareness Africa

In the author's note of my most recent collection, Mirror, I claimed to have laid myself bare in those pages. If I had read PaGidi's Dearest Suicide at the time, I probably would not have made such a bold claim. This book totally, totally, redefines those terms.

It says, "Come, make I gist you as e take happen." You get pulled into the story as it unfolds. The gist comes, spiced with elements of poetry. And it doesn't throw metaphors around, leaving you to figure out what it means; no! It comes at you directly! But not without the sparks and lines of sheer brilliance.

Dearest Suicide will come off as many things to different people. But to me, it's a heartfelt conversation with a new friend, a firsthand account of what really went down, and most of all, it's one of the most detailed histories and accounts of suicide I've read in one piece.

I did not want it to end.

You might begin to wonder if this writer was somehow suggesting that suicide is a logical (maybe even preferred) solution to our problems. If he is romanticizing the concept. Well, that's left for you to determine after you've read.

And that final part? Mysteries! It changed the entire game! I hate that I have to wait so long to read the rest of it... But I'll wait. I'll wait.

PS: What breakfast cannot do does not exist.

PSS: The author warns that you might find his views offensive. I thought it was a ruse till I delved in.

JESS ICA |Hookup Apprentice

There are 171,476 words currently in use in the English dictionary and I don't even know a quarter of these words, but I don't think any or all put together would define what you do or have deep inside

…You're out of this world!

First time I started reading your expressions, and I was like…damn, man is good at picking words I see in my head but my mouth be numb to. I swear this gave me chills.

Your style. The flows. The steadiness, cause you don't fall off a point. I need more of this, cause some are like someone helping out. You get? I find things I can't say in your expressions, and it gives me this feeling of belonging, like being the way I am is just normal.

This is the time I'm enjoying Facebook. Yunnor, like, even when we don't talk, and I read one of them expressions of yours, a poem and a few lines of one's write-up, I feel some sort of belonging yunnor.

You're amazing PaGidi…I'm still wondering how you do this. And very sensitive topics too. I started reading and couldn't stop. So far that I've read your works, yes, they are relatable. More ink!

SIRI |Textile, Delta State University; Fashion Illustrator, Qwho Siri

Went through your profile not quite long…nice poems you've got there. I feel somehow connected to this Expression. But life goes on. Let's just make the best out of it. All is well dear friend.

CHIDI IYKE |Writer; Graphics Designer

I love the way you write. I love the way you connected your thoughts with your present. I love the way you pick out my soul and paste parts of your soul there. Thank you for being a writer.

BARNABAS JNR |Student; Poet

Wow...

This piece pierced my soul, bro.

ERASTUS ADEKUNLE | Writer; Feminist

Gosh! PaGidi, how do you get to do this every time? Wrenching my heart in pieces with every letter, every word, every description and more. You're amazing. Personally, and in the inks.

To be frank, I haven't met a writer like you. And I'm really serious. There's just a way you write, there's something about how you style your words and I just feel like I'm in your mind. Sitting on the chair, watching you compose your Expressions. I see you listening to songs. I feel connected to your essence.

Every time I read from you, I feel like I'm sipping from life's unbridled river of wisdom and inspiration. I'm damn in love with your writing. It's crazy. You make me damn emotional!

You've explored my heart in-depthly. Your personality is one in a million. And your mind, you say it freely and unashamedly. Sometimes, I feel fake. But you're brazen. You tell about your craves, your addiction and you give 'em the….like who cares?

What's the inspiration behind 'Expressions'? I just love the 'interactive' tone and its spice of spontaneity. I think I should go over those stories again. Superb. I love every bit of it. I just find it very unique. Almost diary-like.

You're so real. And great. And amazing. I'm still learning, learning to be me. Not being someone else. For some other people.

I appreciate all your works, and, I'd love to see this Expressions published. Wouldn't it be a great idea?

I love you, PaGidi. The best!

OLUMIDE GLOWVILLE | Digital Marketing Strategist; Convener, Lagos Hangout

Interesting musing.

Intriguing poetry.

I like.

JOY MFON | English Education, University of Uyo

PaGidi, you're unique man. I read every expression you put out here and it's fvking good. Most of them makes me feel like you're talking to me or about me. Your expressions are always amazing. You write well. I love your writing.

Keep doing you. I'm anticipating "Dearest Suicide" though.

ASOLO DANIEL | Editor, AyeteInfo

Pun-star! You're a thespian in disguise. Your choice of language depicts it fa.

ANN BEN | Ghost Writer; Content Creator

How do you do this? How do you manage to write this well?

You write so well.

CLEO DUNSMORE BUCHANAN | Energy Worker, Grama Tortoise Healing Arts

Brilliant my friend!! I love this! Thank you for shining your light!!

VICTOR EFEMENA MAESTRO | Business Development Specialist

God bless the day I found some people's pen. Stained with ingenious ingenuity; the power of which is in its ability to spit out reality in simple forms and give life and palpitations to the hearts of its listeners eyes.

Nice journal. At thine foot, learning secretly. Keep on and I shall be joining in your footsteps someday, probably.

EZE TOCHI PRAISE | Critique Writer

Kai! Omoor! Bro, Poetry doesn't deserve you chaaaa! Am I the only one that feels you should go into content creation?? This is one hell of a Content Write-up…beats over 70% of the entire theories of Poetry! You killed this..swears.

All your works are centered on realities and eventualities as it so affects you. Conversational Poetry at its best! You would pass for a good Poetical Realist.

SARAH AKINTUNDE IMAHIA | Radio Presenter

You daze my imagination with your writing. As I type this comment, you can guess what I am doing, smiling!

Your writings are provocative and highly inspiring. I am still anticipating (3). The "emotional promiscuity" is what is cracking me up . Oyinbo people get name for everything. Well done PaGidi.

BINBOL WILSON | Senior Research Fellow and Academic Writer

I am not expecting any less from the master of thought and poetry himself. Your school of thought is a very rare and unpopular one, but it is good for intellectual exercise. Quite philosophical!

Greatness lives here, PaGidi. I 'throway' salute. But tell me please, was there a time you ever thought of getting married or not getting married at all? Was there a time you ever thought of having children in a marriage or having same out of wedlock?

PRINCE KIRIGBO | Writer

Damn! This is depressingly amazing. You playing with our emotions or what? I like how you think.

MOYINFOLUWA ODUSOLA | Mental Health Advocate

How do your posts escape my newsfeed?

Honestly, I have a lot to catch up on. You write very well.

OLIVER LECHE | Digital Marketer, Social Media Manager

PaGidi…an old man living in a young body and writes from his soul. He writes from personal experiences and they are really deep. He's a Wordsmith and writes fearlessly. When you read this book, you'd understand better. Remember, personal experiences help us relate and resonate more with the writings of the writer. Selah.

AJAYI IFEOLUWA BSc, | Political Science; MSc, Peace Studies and Conflict Resolutions

Dearest Suicide. The title alone sounds like something interesting already.

PaGidi is a senseless boy that is full of sense. The realest writer I've ever mingled with. He writes so effortlessly.

You'll be reading his expressions and it'll feel like he's playfully doing amebo for you. If he had sex yesterday, expect to see it in his Expressions today.

This is gonna be a blockbuster. Fasten your seatbelt y'all. It's about to go down. You'll understand all the lines and relate to the contents as though they happened to you.

REVEREND RACHAEL OLAJUMOKE DISU | Assisting Minister, Foursquare Gospel Church Itoikin Road Zone

PaGidi, I wouldn't say you're incompressible, not at all! But I doff my hat for the ingenuity with which you string words together in conveying your incontestable expressions. This style of yours is very innovative! Keep being original! Welldone!!!

DR. OREOFE WILLIAMS | President, OREOFE FILMS; Arch mentor, City of Talents Worldwide

You are a fantastic writer and as a literary fellow myself, I am extremely proud of your contributions to humanities.

I would have wished someone like you sat before me as a student in my department when I was a University teacher. We need very creative minds like you who have authentic visions and who know why they are in school. I'm glad you proved yourself as an objective writer without an iota of doubting the synthetics and aesthetics that comes with literature.

I might not have read all (your expressions), but the ones I glanced through got me fulfilled that there are fantastic writers around. It actually takes a scholar who is not blinded by sheer piety or religiosity to appreciate your works.

Your art is bold and unapologetically satirical. You don't actually write, you craft. And crafting is what makes a great writer.

Perhaps this could be published, who knows? It also could be a collection.

I deliberately lend my support to your literature publicly and not through the inbox, so that your religious critics would know there are 'Bishops' appreciating your arts (lol).

It's impossible to appreciate literature if you already are biased from the scratch, culturally or religiously. It takes the Wordsworthian tranquillity to see beyond the surface and uncover the metaphors and metonymy that illuminate on the seeming 'metaphysics' of literature. For if a writer doesn't strike someone's anger at the beginning, he won't get him to the end.

I honour you PaGidi and thanks for your consistent honour over the years.

I am exceptionally proud of you and I believe this little comment of mine would help do more for you than a deliberate silence.

Write more!!!!!!!!!!!! And I mean write mooooooooore!!!!!!! Instructors and Institutions are eagerly waiting for your publications.

BRAINIAC WILLIAMS |Graphics Designer; Web Designer

Boss, wallahi you're good with words. I know you know about that already but please take this as a reminder. You're good and there's nothing anyone can do about it. You do you and you do it in a way that's so audacious, unique and fascinating at the same time.

How you usually stitch all of these together should be studied as a 6 unit credit course in the university, honestly.

FUNTO OBADINA LAWAL |Sweden

Your write ups are so captivating.

TES SY |Poetess; Memer

Wow! You are doing well boss! Keep it up.

SALLY KENNETH DADZIE |Author of Roses Aren't Red, Stranger In Lagos

I was scared for a minute but when I began to read, I realized that the thoughts you put down have filled my mind before.

Well captured. Sad and intense. Chilly.

LATEEF MURAINA School Administrator, Livingstone College

Wisdom from the Bard.

ZAINAB ADEKOLE | LGBTQ+ Advocate

You such a brilliant writer!! Our own Shakespear!

OGUNDELE TEMITOPE | Legal Practitioner

It's good that you've found the courage to share your stories through you writing skills……even though I may not have reacted to all your write up or agreed with some of them. I still read all and understand where you are coming from (or so I thought).

I applaud your courage to do this and I ultimately hope that you find peace, healing and every good thing you seek and ditch the thought of suicide.

CHRISTINE ADEKUNLE | UI/UX Designer

I started reading your book and it got to a point I just had to drop the book and think. 80% of youths living in Nigeria has contemplated or entertained the thought of suicide in a way or the other. Love showed you shege and damn you took your time to express it. It must have hurt real bad.

The book showed what it's like to be a student in an institution situated in Nigeria, to be in a one-sided love relationship, life after school and what it's like to face difficulties that's bent on slowing you down.

I was thinking it was going to be a very serious book but it was surprising that I laughed when I read some part. It's nice to see hurt from a guy's point of view. Regardless of the gender, it shows we are all humans after all.

I just read to the place of the girl that loved you but was disturbing you with calls. So I'm thinking…she truly loved you but she didn't speak your love language (s). Maybe I'm wrong sha. Maybe calling frequently was her main love language and maybe you're someone that loves solitude. You wanted a real life thing. Not a virtual kind of love but a physical something. Not the "I miss you" "I miss you too" kind of love. I can totally relate.

But why the fuck did you fucked the relationship? That lady loved you so much!

And why did you end the book that way? I'm waiting for part two o.

DHANIEL FAKUNMOJU | Microbiology, Lagos State University

Guuuuy I hate you. You're just ending every chapter with me expecting more on the story or chapter. Your writing is infectious and gives don't-drop-it vibes.

The fact you made it one chapter, story, next chapter, facts, made the book just make more sense. You brought the reader to another mind frame from the previous chapter. The story is about suicide, but you didn't over emphasize on suicide…you used facts and figures to tell a story from your stand point. You're talking about yourself but you didn't lose sight on the topic.

Guy I swear, you yourself you don't know how much this is going to fuck people's mental state. The more I read this book, the more I realize "13 Reasons Why" was very structured.

Meanwhile, the one girl that loved you, where is she? Make we go shoot shot again.

EMMANUEL OJODUN | Brand Strategist; Graphics Designer

Common bro! You had me in mind when writing this book. Just reading the prologue and I am screaming already. No little wonder we could connect easily.

Currently at page 60, and all I can say is that we had the same love issues…it is just at different times and seasons of our lives.

ELAIGWU PHILGRACE | Legal Practitioner

This is one way to relax from the whole seemingly bedlam going on in the country. PaGidi is an intentional writer, picks every word and phrase purposefully.

This guy is real, especially in a world where people hide their downsides.

I had a good time reading, at many times I literally laughed out. It was fun. It was worth my time. I admire your audacity and also love the way you are living, not existing.

You sha like to leave us wondering and asking rhetorical question or raising arguments if the topic is raised. Lolz, that's what makes you, you.

I know there is a part 2 and I look forward to it. I honestly cannot wait for part 2.

OYEWOLE ADEJOKE |Teenager

Today, I was bored, in my feelings, just like I was living in my future today, I was fucked up. I read DEAREST SUICIDE today, it was wow. Thank you for giving me a space in your life and most especially giving me privilege to read the book, it was lovely. Thank you.

TGERALDO |Football Enthusiast

Hey man, when all things are said and done, we need to talk. Been reading your book since 2 days....very thoughtful, insightful and painful. An emotional rollercoaster.

This book is coming at a time in my life I am at a crossroads. Right now. Anyways...been reading your other Facebook post before…trying to window through your creative mind.

ANGELMICHAEL KEHINDE OLAWALE |Lead Steward, Young, Original and Useful

I see PaGidi as one who has the task to build the ruins in the mind of many who are trodden by the many fallacies poised by the dampened system that has caged our spirit, soul, and body. Thank you for all you do to liberate many from the chains of madness.

EMMANUEL ONOWARO (DR. FLUID) │Professional Counselling at Attitude Development International

This right here... Absorbent reading...Just soaking up the pieces of another's experiences... A man's life cut in little bite-sized bits and shared with the world... That's how PaGidi makes me feel sometimes.

This page is home to me. For a crazed Casanova lover, both for his adventurous life and his highly epistemic memoirs (some critics say it's laced with imaginative fiction - true or not, you can't help but be thrilled), PaGidi comes to mind as a unique and free-willed expressive.

BTW, there's no comparison here. They are both great men in their own rights!!!

It's how you read PaGidi Expressions sometimes and all the reactions on Facebook match how you feel, but you have to choose just one, and you can't explain how you feel exactly because it's the opening of dams in your system.

Absorbent reading is what I have for your works. It just hit me strongly how calling them "works" somehow externalizes you from these words, which is contrary to what I really feel when I read Expressions. To be soaked up in the vividly captivating truth of another, to read over and over again to fully (if at all possible) taste of the various raw emotions and feelings that words have so marvellously tried to capture.

This is the recognition of a man who has grabbed the reins of life and has chosen to steer the horse wherever he (the rider) leads. Such open courage and daunting brazenness in the face of a people who thrive by deceptive cowardice and misaligned malicious boldness gives me the thrills and prompts me onwards on the journey of 'enrealment'.

It's in how you take me through the journey of your experiences and I'm at the end of an entry, sitting and staring while my brain digests what's been read. PaGidi take me over and over through these rollercoasters. I'll be your turnioniown specimen.

Can't even talk about this, as with many other Expressions... It would be like adding water to already prepared yoghurt...Your expressions are that raw.

And it's in the clarity of thoughts (although I'm almost certain the many times one would spend hours or days thinking of how best to start off with writing about the bouncing thoughts in the head). You know how you can be confused on writing about your confusion and you end up writing confused thoughts that leave the readers more confused, but we rest in the knowledge that the summation of all the confusion is beautiful?

The things you do to my mind bro...You know how some say "don't fuck with my mind?" Never listen to them when with your Expressions or with me... Do all the fuckery you can with it and leave me in perpetual braingasms.

And as regards this Expression, this dilemma is as familiar as skin to bone. And the questions that come up as one approaches that transitory gate...do you do that thing where you finally decide to throw your hands off the wheels and see where the car auto-drives you to?

Again, no comparison. If I have a compiled copy of PG's memoir, be sure it's one book that will NEVER leave my shelf.

TABLE OF CONTENT

QUICK DISCLAIMER

The content you are about to read contains extremely-provocative words, languages, views, and opinions that may come out as disturbing and offensive to your person, faith, lifestyle, and beliefs.

Be borne in mind that the words herein remain the intellectual property of **PaGidi Expressions**, and has no affiliation with, or should be misinterpreted to be forming part of the words, opinions, or content of any prior or future writer, author, publisher or whosoever.

This appeal is made with good conscience: because words are very powerful, and human opinions are very delicate; as such, they ought to be handled with utmost care, caution, and understanding.

However, I as a person handle human words + opinions with the highest form of disregard, without any apology to anyone.

Readers are thus **<u>strongly advised</u>** to make conscious effort to decide whether or not to consider the contents therein.

The names of real characters were included for proper reference, so as not to serve as a fictional tale or anything close to it. ***<u>Their identity shouldn't in any way be construed as representing whatsoever image represented or role played in my life.</u>***

Many parts, lines of thought and expressions might have changed in perspective or their present-day reality; but here I am writing out how I felt at the very point in time of their presence in my life.

<u>They each have their stories to tell. Here is mine.</u>

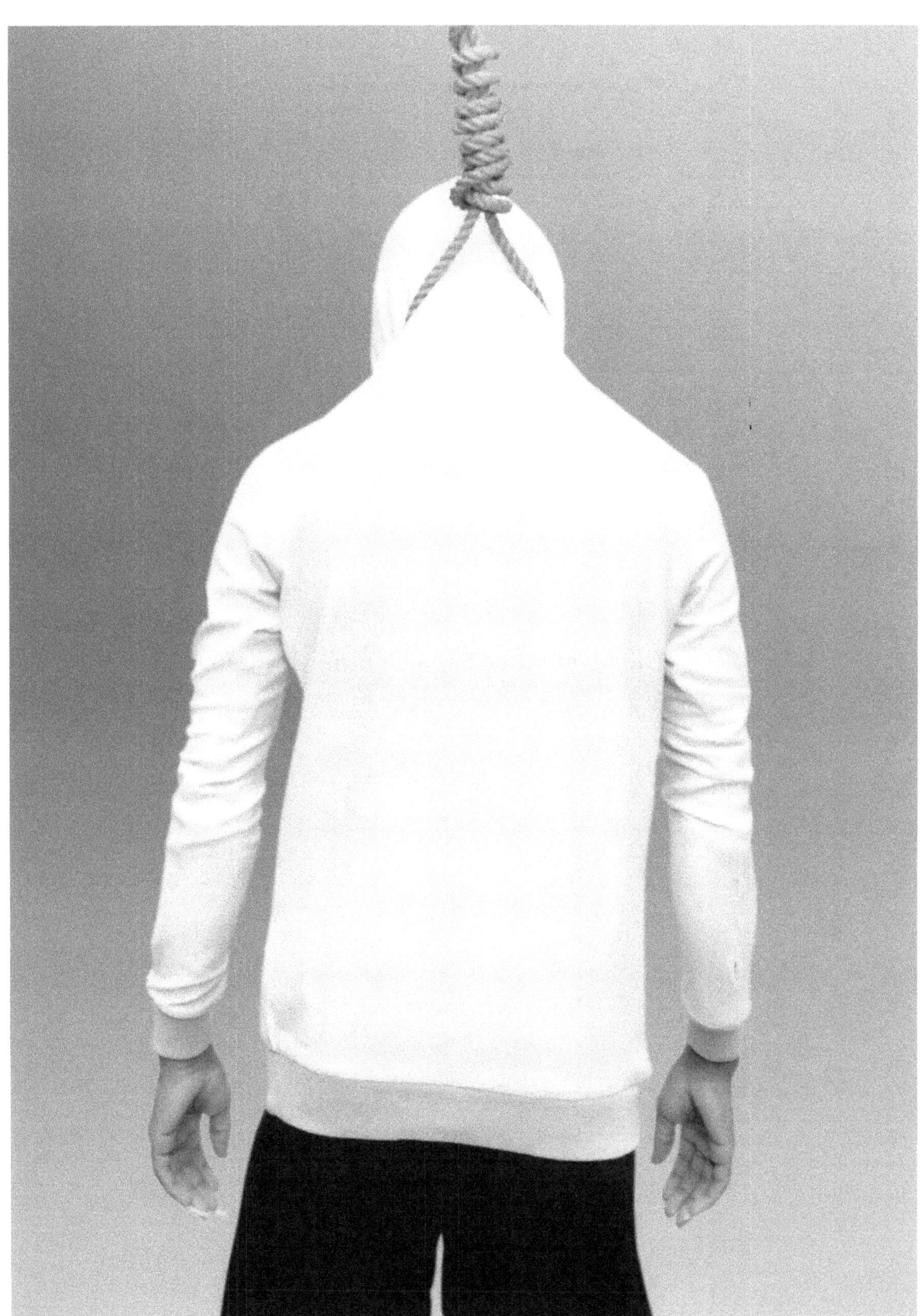

The Mysterious Saga Continues…

Expressions:
Dearest Suicide

Part 11: Little Angels

Everyone can have one thing or the
Other to say when it comes to suicide,
But it won't change the narrative that
Many-a-youth are battling with quite
A number of problems they can't talk
To anyone about.

Even to themselves.

Sometimes, believing death
To be the only way out of
Such problem.

In the pursuit for happiness, there's
The struggle to be loved, the search
For a job, the quest for academic
Success, the chase of money.

And the constant need to project
Ourselves as the persons we're
Not on social media, or peppered
By what we see people post.

But, Dearest Suicide, the number of
Count charges against you for killing

Young minds and creative souls, has
Been way so/too alarming!

That, even if I were to be
Your lawyer, I'll back outta
The case!

My dear, they said you've killed
A lot of teenagers!

It's so sad!

A little lad who hadn't even lived
Up to a decade on earth plunged
To his death in horrific fashion.

Question marks could have been
Raised as to why the little lad, who
Was just eight years old, would even
Think of jumping off the window of his
House to die in the very first instance.

But, for a lad who had been regularly
Beaten by his parents for one little
Mistake or another, he could have

Been easily forgiven for making
Such a choice.

Especially after visiting a psychologist
For counselling several times without
Positive result.

Then a nineteen-year-old stepped
In front of a moving train, after
Becoming overwhelmed by his
Battles with cocaine.

And gambling.

The teenager left a voicemail for his
Parents, saying *"see you on the other
Side",* before throwing himself in front
Of the train.

Prior to his troubles with drugs and
Gambling, he had been going through
A whole lot, while suffering from a
Breakdown in his emotional life.

Due to the reality he had to come to

Terms with regarding his relationship
With his girlfriend.

Seeking mental health support, he was
Reassured that he was recovering well
And gradually getting better.

But this didn't stop him from ending his life.

Up until his death, he was an avid
Footballer who had a normal and
Happy childhood, and had excelled
Well at his school.

And even though he talked openly
About his drug use and relationships,
YOU still allowed him to jump off the
Moving train.

How about the teenager you induced
To kill himself at a children's park, just
Because of a fall out he had with his
Mom?

Kyle Hartshorne, also nineteen, had

Moved out of the family home, writing
About suicide on his Facebook posts.

Before he was later found dead the
Morning after, by a maintenance
Worker who was simply carrying
Out a routine check in the area.

Kyle still seemed so okay and happy
Prior to the day you took him away;
But beneath the smiles he tried to
Mask his face with, there were many
Things he was hiding about himself.

After High School, Kyle found it difficult
Getting a job, and had to settle for what
He was most passionate about.

Wearing female clothes and makeups.

He was soon able to make a quick impact
On everyone he met, being loud with his
New personality, and always loving to be
At the centre of attention.

Sometimes he would post something on
Facebook about his makeup; other times,
He would post about his mental health.

But since he left no suicide note before
Leaving, we can only guess (through his
Facebook posts about mental health),
That the world became too much for
Him.

Possibly, people couldn't understand
His kind of person/personality, neither
Could they understand why a guy would
Choose to wear female clothes and make
Ups.

So many issues he was struggling
With. Things you chose to capitalize
On, that caused him to end his life.

Similar to the story of Kyle, eighteen
Year old Cameron Haswell hung himself
While wearing a female jumpsuit.

Due to his hidden gender identity struggles.

Cameron was silently suffering in his head
And didn't open up about his struggles, and
It is believed that he took his life to send a
Message about his gender battles.

He was confused about his gender identity,
Was unable to define or accept who he was
As a person, and wasn't feeling comfortable
Talking to anyone about it.

Tragic.

Surprisingly, I didn't know that these
Sort of struggles existed until I came
Across the story of Cameron.

It was then it then dawned on me that,
While so many people are given birth
To as boys or girls, some others are
Terribly struggling with the social
Construct of being a boy or girl.

And they just wished they could
Take away that gender in them
And act as the opposite specie

Of who they are defined as.

Or become gender fluid.

Because that's who they think or
Feel or believe they really are.

It came as a positive news (for me personally)
When the family came out to speak, following
The death of Cameron, to raise awareness of
Mental health and gender identity.

"I think he was very confused", his mom
Said, adding, *"A lot of girls and boys need
To know it is not something to be ashamed
Of, and it shouldn't be a secret.*

*"One of the most painful things to contend
With, is that as a family we are open minded
And accepting and would never have made
Cameron feel anything other than supported
And loved in any decision he needed to make."*

Did you read that? Cameron's family were
(Or are) open minded, and accepting, and

Supporting, and loving.

Irrespective of the decision he made
About his sexual orientation and
Gender identification.

Now, even though these people preferred
To call it "gender identity struggles", I would
Rather call it "gay acceptance identity", or
The one commonly known – LGBTQ+

Heard there's a new now - LGBTQIA+

And you know, a lot of humans have argued
For and against the gay community in recent
Years, with certain movies like "Sex Education"
And "How To Get Away With Murder" helping
Us appreciate the gay structure in a well-loved
And understanding manner.

I even discovered there are more
Than seventy gender or sexual
Identifications globally!

Nonetheless, question marks have still

Been raised on the parts of parents over
What they would do if and when they
Find out that their child comes out as
Being a gay or lesbian or transgender
Or queer or anything so confusedly
Posed that has no popular definition.

More like, can you accept your child
To call himself as gay or herself as a
Lesbian?

Can you allow your child to be
A Daniel Anthony, Jay Bugatti,
Bobrisky or James Brown?

And I'm not even throwing the
Question to the Generation X
Or Millennials, I'm asking you
Gen Z folks.

When you start having your children,
Will you be okay allowing them identify
With whatever more confused gender
Identification/classification that would
Have been existing by then??

Well, I'll leave that for you to ponder upon.

However, (speaking generally now), if you
Are yet to understand the complexities of
Life as it relates to suicide, then you've got
To read about this girl who was so determined
To take her own life, to the extent that she
Marked the date of her death on her calendar.

Stealth!

Alicia Sidebotham, described as a bright and
Strong-willed teenager, was found hanged in
The woods, after she left her family a note
Saying she was going to die anyway.

Some guts huh?!

In the months leading up to her
Death, Alicia had self-harmed on
Three separate occasions, all in
A bid to kill herself.

It was so bad that she was moved to
Children And Adult Mental Health

Services (CAMHS) for some months.

After spending time in hospital, undergoing
Scheduled therapy and prescribed medication,
Alicia was discharged from the facility,
And then moved into her own flat.

Where she successfully killed herself.

In the aftermath of her death, her flat
Was searched and an empty bottle of
Vodka + a small snap-bag containing
Traces of white powder was found.

It was there they also found a six-paged
Suicide note she had written about how
She wanted to die, with the date of her
Death marked on the calendar in her
Kitchen.

She was nineteen.

Here's what her mom had to say
About Alicia's death:

"When she was 15, she had gone to some
Woods and had thought about hanging
Herself, but she took a photo of her
Brother with her and said that
Stopped her from doing it.

"In November 2016, she took an overdose
Of paracetamol. She took herself to the
Hospital because I think she knew she
Had not taken enough.

"In January 2017, she took another
Dose of paracetamol, which was
The serious attempt.

"She was vomiting and came
Downstairs and told me what
She had done.

"It was just her thought processes,
She thought she was going to die
Anyway in the future.

"Nobody could change her rationale
And what she thought in her mind.

"She has asked everyone not to
Feel sad for her."

End of talk.

Then there's Noa Pothoven, a seventeen-
Year-old rape victim from the Netherlands,
Who died at her home, after starving herself
To death in a bid to end her life.

In a final social media post a day before
Her death, Noa made her decision public.

"I deliberated for quite a while whether
Or not I should share this, but decided
To do it anyway.

"Maybe this comes as a surprise to some,
Given my posts about hospitalization, but
My plan has been there for a long time,
And is not impulsive.

"I will get straight to the point:
Within a maximum of ten days,
I will die.

"After years of battling and fighting,
I am drained.

"I have quit eating and drinking for a
While now, and after many discussions
And evaluations, it was decided to
Let me go, because my suffering is
Unbearable."

Wahala!

Before her death, Noa had written an
Autobiography about her life, which
She titled 'Winning or Learning'.

The book talked about her battles with
Mental illness, wherein she was molested
At age eleven, before being raped at age
Fifteen.

As a result of the abuse, she suffered
From post-traumatic stress disorder
(PTSD), depression and anorexia.

Noa said she wanted her book to help

Vulnerable youngsters who struggle
With life, arguing that Netherlands
Doesn't have specialized institutions
Or clinics where teenagers can go to
For physical or psychological aid.

And then again, there's the case of a
Sixteen-year-old girl who jumped to
Her death hours after she was sexually
Assaulted at her school.

Mya Vizcarrondo-Rios jumped off the roof
Of her home in New York, after two boys
Allegedly forced her to perform oral sex
On them.

Grossss!!

The oral sex happened, and sadly
For her, she was then teased by
Some classmates who found out
About the incident.

Mya then left school earlier than
Scheduled, only to leap off the

34-storey building of her home.

Her backpack was still on her
When her body was found.

There's also this *"mad oh!"* story of a
Sixteen-year-old girl who was found
Dead at the bottom of a three-storey
Shop in Malaysia.

After carrying out a live or die
Poll on Instagram.

"Really Important, Help Me Choose D/L".

Horrifyingly, 69 percent of the people
Who responded told the girl to choose
D (Die).

And she chose it.

The final result of the 24 hour poll,
Though, had 88 percent of people
Urging her to choose L (Live).

By that time, she was already dead.

She had earlier posted a message
On Facebook saying *"WANNA
QUIT FUCKING LIFE I'M
TIRED"*.

That's just a little of the things that
These little angels and vulnerable
Youngsters have been going through
In the past couple of years and since
Forever.

But these guys aren't alone in the
Struggle to live and in the quest
For a happy and peaceful life.

Even as a teenager myself, I received
A number of moments that proved
Life to be difficult and questioned
The existence of God in the pursuit
Of my happiness.

And just like everyone's story is
Unique in its own way, mine was

Beyond what I could just summarize
By saying "I suffered while growing up."

(I mean, who didn't??)

Mine wasn't a case of poverty
Though, it was a question of
Existential confusions.

Between the age of eleven to seventeen,
There were a number of difficulties I tried to
Cope with, while being confused about what
Life meant and why things were happening
To me in the fucked-up way they were
Happening.

Such that, at the age of eighteen when I
Ought to round up my teenage life and
Start enjoying my adulthood, I already
Got fed up of life and felt like dying.

Or killing myself: just in case
Death wasn't ready to come.

The ways and patterns of living introduced

To me by the systems and cultures of this
World just wasn't working for someone
Like me.

For everything they had been telling me
To do as a sign of being human, I found
Much more struggle trying to live with
'Em.

And even considered myself an alien
To the things I ought to be human to.

Here's why.

For every life I was trying
To live, I struggled to live.

For every air I was trying to
Inhale, I struggled to breathe.

For every pattern I was being
Taught to tow, I struggled to
Flow.

For every way I was trying

To go, I struggled to grow.

And when it came to matters
Of God, religion, and the state
Of my spirituality, I struggled
To keep up with the pace.

It just felt like I wasn't going
To make heaven, no matter
How spiritual I tried to be.

Which was a tougher struggle in itself,
Because it was difficult for me to voice
Out that even though I am Christian and
The first born child of a Reverend, the
Christian life just wasn't made for me.

It was seriously annoying to imagine
That I had to be doing the Christianity
Stuff, because my parents are one, or
Because I was born into it, or because
Of what people would say if I do other-
Wise.

When I knew deep within me that

I just wasn't coping with the system,
And there were other things I desired
To get myself involved in/with.

Yes, I hated the idea of being called
A sinner, and as a teenager, I didn't
Have the confidence to scream out
"I'm not interested in being a child
Of God again!!!"

I just couldn't adapt to anything
At all, I always found myself at
The bottom of every definition,
Struggling to fit into their meaning.

And rather than being the king
Of my castle, I became a prey
In my own kingdom.

I always considered myself the odd
One of the lot, and I didn't see my
Being-the-odd one as something I
Could alter.

Even amongst the ones I was thinking

Or believing were my friends, I found
Myself in a constant struggle to fit into
Their circle.

JJC. Butti pikin. Omo get inside.

I was everything!

And what about girlfriend??

I'm not sure if any girl was ready to
Be my girlfriend, but I was so sure
That I didn't have the nerve or liver
To ask a girl out.

Based on the way I was brought up.

I remember those days in my secondary
School when I had to struggle with the
Idea of having a crush on someone but
Not being able to talk to her about my
Feelings.

The idea of seeing a girl I like, but not
Being able to say anything apart from

A *"hi"*, and talking to them in my mind
Instead of talking to them in person.

And behaving as though I'm already
Dating them, when I haven't even
Said a word about how my feelings
Is making me to feel iranu for them.

"Them", because they were always
Many. Not just one girl. And I was
Having feelings for them all!

It was emotionally draining + disturbing
For me: in that, I knew I had feelings for
These girls (that oftentimes made me
Have an erection in awkward spaces
In public), but didn't know how to
Talk to any one of the girls about
It.

Because I didn't want to be seen
As a player or a bad boy.

What could have been the reason for
This fear? Could I have ever known?

I don't know. But I felt bad about it
Each time I remembered that I liked
A girl, but couldn't say anything to
Her about it.

While watching her being swept off
Her feet by another guy that wouldn't
Have been able to take care of her the
Way I would have so desired.

Plus, I'd already been told some
Things about boy-girl relationship.

That having a girlfriend as a teenager
Is a bad thing for a child of God and
Portrays you as a wayward child to
Your family.

Being a Pastor's son, I could easily agree
I had a great burden on my neck, and I
Didn't want to find myself in any form
Of compromising situation or position.

All the same, I knew deep within me
That I couldn't do without not having

An imaginary girlfriend, and this killed
Me and my feelings towards having a
Real girlfriend every new day.

No, not imaginary girlfriend as in
Imaginary girlfriend, but imagining
That I am already dating the girl I
Like, whom I'm not even bold
Enough to talk to.

Phew!

To say the least, I didn't even know how
To ask a girl out – a condition I still find
Myself in constant struggle with till this
Very second.

Such that, once I mistakenly become
Close to any girl that's equally giving
Me some level of attention, I begin to
Imagine things.

And even start seeing us walking
Down the aisle "in holy matrimony".

But to start up a conversation with her?

Oh-puh-lease, count me out.

Guys around me were talking to girls
With all ease, gusto and confidence,
And that was something I found almost
Impossible to do.

I couldn't tell them, *"well, although*
You are a very beautiful girl, I have
No clue on how to talk to you."

But I would have said this thing to
Her in my mind, and would have
Had an hour or two talk from that
Little pick up line.

ALL IN MY MIND!!!!

Yeah, back then, mental pressure wasn't
Something anyone talked about – it's
Either you are "a good kid" or "a bad
Kid".

However, what I didn't know was that
I was undergoing different bouts of
Multiple + complex social anxieties.

It became so unbearable for me; and
With no outer means of expressing the
Emotions, the thought processes and
Burdens began to take its toll on me.
So, what did I do?

I helped myself with an external
Fantasy only me could enjoy and
Find pleasure in.

Pornography. Masturbation.
And social media sites.

Things the mainstream society now
Define as sexual addiction – which
By the way was part of what was
Giving me headache back then.

I mean the definition, and how it
Was embarrassingly shamed on
Us.

Could it have been okay to say I wasn't
Addicted to these things, and had only
Made it become my way of surviving
In the midst of the pressures I had?

Well, I can't say.

But the more I aged, the more I found
Myself getting tired of many things and
Everything all together.

Mentoring? Counselling? Advising?
Preaching? I no longer cared about
Being under those things.

I literally stopped doing whatever I had
Been told was important to my life, and
Sat down to watch and see how things
Would unfold on its own.

Yes, I was already giving up, drifting
Towards the path of suicide, as the
Weight of depression began to eat
Deep into my soul.

Not even the question of morality could
Stand in my way; I became dead to any
Talk concerning sexual sin or any of its
Accompanying iniquities.

I also became tired of being the good
Kid or acting like a responsible child,
When it added nothing to my life or
Exposure or account balance.

With every act of godliness, purity, and
Morality I previously tried to uphold, I
Found myself becoming the guy suffering
From a religion I knew nothing about.

Instead of living my life and
Enjoying the life out of it.

I also became tired of love.
By love, I refer to whatever name it's
So called, wherein the end result is
Wedding.

Abi marriage.

I cared less about what marriage had to
Offer: the who and when and all theories
And postulations attached to datingnology.

Especially the gospel of sex and virginity.

I didn't believe in wedding anymore, and
I gave up on my previous hope or plan of
Getting married to the love of my life.

What is even "love of my life"?

Where is the love?

And do I even have a life???

I no longer cared whether anyone loved me
Or not: was not even ready to be deceived
Or cajoled into loving anyone anymore.

I could not even stand the activities of
The church as well, so I chose to opt out
Of the system for the time being and see
How life would be "without God in it."

There's a way of life that has always
Been annoyingly annoying to certain
Teenage Christians:

School, Home, Church, Home,
School, Home, Church, Home,
School, Home, Church, Home,
School, Home, Church, Home.

No other life – except few visits
To family friends, cousins, and
Birthday parties.

For the parents of these teenagers,
This is the ideal + perfect life to live.

But to these teenagers, this is only
The beginning of a growing problem
That'll keep on following them into
Adulthood.

Until they become a usefully useless adult
Who has only been living according to the
Plans and desires of his/her parents, pastors,
Mentors, and so on.

Aptly said, they have grown up to
Become a good child: no exposure,
No experience, no maturity, nothing
At all.

Just a good-for-nothing child!

Simply vibes and insha allah.

So, some teenagers would always think of
Suicide: because they are teenagers, and
They don't like or appreciate the way and
Manner in which they are/were raised.

Expressions:

Dearest Suicide

Part 12: Teen Age Crisis

As previously established and possibly
Now understood, one of the age group
Of suicidal activities prevalent in our
Time involves that of teenagers.

Teenage suicide is so serious and such
A growing concern that some of us fail
To understand the emotional turbulence
And difficulties ravaging the average
Teen age child.

Oftentimes, when teenagers elect to die
By suicide, one of the first set of things
People say is *"How come?"*

Then, *"What happened?"*

And some other times, we take the long
Route by asking: *"What was the person
Thinking of?"*

But with the kind of society we live in, what
Couldn't have happened to a teenager who
Is deeply struggling to have a life + breathe
A breath of survival?

And fuck all of the talk about peer pressure,
Social vices, moral decadence, and the other
Terminological bullshits we bash these guys
With.

Because like I said, all we do is rant
When we aren't the ones wearing
The pant.

So, why do teenagers commit suicide?
Have you ever asked yourself that?

I'm sure you countlessly have.

I have too. And sometimes, it's
Pretty worrisome to get the right
Answers when I think about the
"Why".

Trying to wonder why someone so
Young and handsome/beautiful,
Would suddenly kill himself or
Herself without reason.

When there's a lot in life to live for.

But, one thing that's most paramount
Is that, being a teenager is by no means
An easy life to live.

Adulthood may look tough, but teenage
Life is a crazy ride of hiccups and bullshits.

The reasons why young people feel
Suicidal are often complex, but we
Know that traumatic experiences
At a young age can be gruesome.

Often times leading to depression.

You might have not realized it, but it's
A very hard life to live in when you're
Still being called a teenager.

It's a very thick web that distinguishes
The innocent childhood from what you
Call "an experienced" adulthood.

However, we focus so much on adulthood
That sometimes, we fail to recognize, accept,
And/or acknowledge that the teenage life is

What gave birth to whatever experience we
Now have in the so-called adulthood.

Not the other way round.

Sure, it can be a time of tremendous
Possibilities and opportunities, but it
Can also be a period of endless stress
And immeasurable worries.

It actually is.

In the teen age life, there are lots of
Pressures to cope with: from family,
Academic, social, and personal
Pressures.

The pressure to act responsibly and be a
Good child in your family, the pressure to
Perform well academically and "carry first
Position" at the end of each term.

Then the pressure to fit in socially, and
The pressure to understand personal
Cum life struggles.

Such as problems or pressures at school,
Difficulties at home, issues, changes and
Disagreements with (or withdrawal from)
Friends, and so on, and so forth.

A fight with a friend might not seem like
A big deal to you in the larger scheme of
Things, but for a teen, it means the whole
World to them.

And oftentimes feels like an immense struggle.

A major family change or conflict such as
Siblings moving out, relocating to a new
Town, parental divorce or separation can
Also have a significant effect in the life of
A teenager.

More importantly, the teen age is a time of
Sexual identity and relationship discovery,
Where teens worry about their sexuality,
What virginity really means, if sex is good
For them or not, what sperm, menstruation
And pregnancy entails, and the state of
Their heart when it deals with matters

Of love and the crushes that comes with
It.

Wondering if their feelings and attractions
Are normal, if they will be loved and accepted
By the person they feel attracted to, and if
They are ready to have a boyfriend/girlfriend
Or not.

Meanwhile, parents, religious leaders,
And relationship counsellors and mentor
Groups are practically saying otherwise
And controlling how their bodies should
Feel.

In a way that's too confusing
For them to believe.

It gets worse when these teenagers
Have to go through, encounter, or
Suffer a devastating heartbreak, all
Because of a relationship breakup.

And there are still greater issues like,
Dealing with bisexuals, homosexuality,

Lesbianism, amongst others, in a family
Or community that's so unsupportive or
A hostile school environment that frowns
At such "acts".

These things can as well be
A problem for teenagers.

Other struggles come in the form
Of body changes and body images.

These body changes include and
Involves everything that has to do
With the adolescent life and the
Puberty occurrences as illustrated
Earlier.

While body images include changes in
Thoughts, actions, dispositions, stress,
Confusions, fear, feelings of alienation,
High self-doubt, low self-esteem and
Concerns about how you look and the
Need for some level of independence.

An independence that often times conflicts

With the rules and expectations set by the
Parents, teachers, and every other circle
Of influence.

Trying to reach an ideal that feels impossible
To achieve leaves them with problems that
Seem too hard or embarrassing to overcome.

They feel disappointed in themselves
And feel they are a disappointment
To others.

Some teenagers equally have learning problems
Or attention challenges that makes it difficult for
Them to comprehend things, giving them much
More pressure to succeed.

It also takes the form of other problems
Like difficulty sleeping, difficulty eating,
Being cranky and irritable, chronic sadness,
Bitterness, withdrawal from regular activities,
Violence and/or rebellious behavior.

Or just crying unexplainably.

These things, a times, leads to unusual neglect
Of personal appearance, persistent boredom,
Difficulty concentrating, and consumption of
Heavy alcohol or hard drugs.

Just to chase what is pursuing them,
Or just to kill what is killing them.

And for teens who have additional problems
To deal with, such as living in violent or abusive
Environments – especially sexually - and those
Who are victims of bullying, it can feel even
More difficult trying to cope with life.

And are at greater risks of suicidal thoughts.
It is said that one in five teenagers have
Contemplated suicide because of bullying
At school, and more than half of them said
They have been bullied in some other places.

Being bullied has made them feel
Anxious, while some have not been
Able to sleep at night as a result of
Sexual harassment.

With some justifiably missing school
And some others changing schools or
Becoming home schooled.

Just because of the fears they now have.

Chris Elmore, a political figure in England,
Revealed during a video interview that he
Considered taking his own life after bullies
At school kicked him until he bled, urinated
On his PE clothes and spat all over his face.

"There were points when I was 13/14
Years old when I would have happily
Not have been here anymore.

"I googled taking my own life. I thought
It would have been easier than dealing
With the bullies."

Elmore said.

For some teens, these issues can be
Very unsettling, when combined with
Their life events, and can be difficult

And draining if it goes on for too long.

For some other teens, these things
Lead one to chronic anxiety, mental
Health challenges, and some form
Of aggravated depression.

Then for those unable to handle the
Crisis or control the situation, or take
Care of the depression they are going
Through, it inadvertently leads them
To looking up to suicide as a solution.

In the same manner, teens who have
Experienced a recent loss of a family
Member, a friend, or a classmate (who
Committed suicide), have the tendency
Of being vulnerable to suicidal thoughts.

This is a truth. This is a fact. This is a reality.

As such, understanding depression in teens
Is very important - since it can look different
From the commonly held beliefs on what
Depression really means, or what suicide

Really means.

As you can see from their daily life struggles.
A teenager with depression may feel there's
No other way out of his or her problem, no
Other way to escape from emotional pain,
And/or no other way to communicate their
Dissatisfying unhappiness.

Thus, seeking a way out through…

…yeah, you gerrit.

But you see, Africans parents would
Always be Africans; and the Nigerian
Ones would always show themselves.

When this sort of information becomes
Common knowledge to us (depression
And suicide), rather than becoming sort
Or understanding and empathetic with
These things, we always find a way to
Fuck things up.

Most especially by pouncing into the space

Of these teenagers, and demanding that they
"Tell me why these things were happening to
You and you couldn't open up to me about it?"

Sometimes, you even carry out these talks
Or discussions with these teenagers in a way
That only brings out the bitter memories in
Their heads.

Thereby making them
Hate you all the more.

African mentality = One hundred and five.
Emotional Intelligence = A fucking zero!

What's even this silly idea about
Parents always feeling good that
Things are going "good" for their
Children?

Why don't they have the least of
Ideas that their children are so
Drained by the thought of them
Having to "act good" to their parents?

Why don't they have the least of
Ideas that their children are tired
Of feeling good in a world that's
Actually crashing down on them?

It's fucked up. It's crazy. It's stupid.

And it's a thing of pride, to only think
Of the "good things" that's supposed
To happen to your child, and get sad,
Disappointed, or even angry when bad
Things happen to them.

I mean, as a parent, has bad thing
Never happened to you while you
Were at their age?

So, what's the fuss about
Bringing down the world
On them?

Why not also allow these supposed
Children live their life and experience
Their experience while they still have
Time?

Rather than being all selfish and
Over protective over 'nothing'.

And if you're only going to celebrate their
Life when good things happen (just because
Of the image you have to project/protect in
The society), what should those who don't
Get the opportunity to be "good" do?

What should they celebrate? How
Should they cope? How should
They handle their situation?

What should they do?

Because, I know how good you compare
Your own children in thanksgiving over
Theirs (saying *"I thank God my children*
Aren't in the hospital, prison, didn't fail,
Are still virgins, and bla bla bla").
As if your children are any better
Than those who don't have it good.

Yes, the tragedy of a teenager dying as a

Result of suicide can be so devastating to
Family members and friends of the victim.

Leaving them not only grief stricken,
But also developing feelings of guilt.

With many wondering where they went
Wrong, asking if they missed something,
And wondering if they could have done
Anything to prevent the young individual
From turning to suicide.

We should understand that it's normal to
Feel guilty and to question how this could
Have happened, but it's also important to
Realize that you might never get answers
To the questions you ask.

No matter how much you
Try or how hard you cry.

Sometimes, teens who make a suicidal
Attempt - or who die as a result of the
Attempt - seem to give no clue before
Hand.

And some other times, they actually
Do, if you look at their circle closely.

Most teens interviewed after making
A suicidal attempt say that they did it
Because they were trying to escape
From a situation that was impossible
To deal with.

Or to get a lasting peace/relief from
A really bad set of thoughts/feelings.

They might have not desired to die as
Much as they wanted to escape from
What was going on in their life; but as
Much as they didn't want to do what
They didn't feel like doing, dying felt
Like the only way out of their problem.

Some adults feel that kids who say
They are going to kill themselves
"Are just looking for attention".

And some other times, they are
Being stupidly hushed, shushed,

Bullied, abused, insulted, and
Silenced on social media.

Be it Facebook, Instagram,
Twitter, Snap Chat, Tik Tok,
Or what have you.

Just because they are actually trying
To voice out the pains in their hearts,
In the little-and-only way they feel
They can.

The discrimination meted on teenagers
Is so dehumanizing that sometimes, we
Become so proud and foolish to admit
That we also were once teenagers who
Did "rebellious" things.

The same rebellious things we are
Accusing these young and growing
Minds of.

So, by way of adjudication, what moral
Justification do we then have for rashly
And unjustly lashing out on weak and

Fragile teenage minds who are only
Trying to find their feet in the circle
Of life?

Especially for a silly country like Nigeria
Where certain godly/religious parents
Feel they know it all, and that it is an
Aberration for their child to think of
Committing suicide.

People think they can see it coming.
They think it comes in patterns. And
Sometimes, they even spiritualize it
By saying *"it can't happen to my*
Child in Jesus name."

What makes your child different
From other children?

You know it's out there, but just
Because it doesn't affect your child,
The trauma doesn't hit home.

And most times, when topical issues
Like this come up in public squares,

We oftentimes try our best in patching
The stories and ignoring the real cause
Of action.

Because, rather than discuss the problem
At full length and across board, we make
Use of hypothetical stories and creative
Illusions to tackle real problems travailing
The lives of what these teenagers are going
Through.

Here's what I mean.

So, Bola is going through masturbation
In a way that is disturbing her teenage
Life and messing up her mind.

Now, rather than help Bola understand
What she is going through, and bring her
Out in her story so that Esther can read
And be aware that she is not alone, we
Make up a story and put Sandra as the
Name of the person going through the
Stuff.

Then use one moral, biblical, or Jesus talk
To illustrate how bad it is to masturbate,
And how God came to cleanse "Sandra"
Of her sins, after confessing her sins and
Giving her life to Christ.

Now, both Bola who is really suffering
The 'mess' and Esther, who ought to read
And realize she's not alone, now have to
Look for a way of giving their life to Christ
So as to get the healing "Sandra" got.

Really???

Meanwhile, Christians are masturbating
In full flesh and blood, but don't open up
About it because it's not supposed to be
Heard of or discussed in a public space.

That our doctrines don't agree with,
Accept, or acknowledge certain things
As good shouldn't make us hide away
From the realities in them!

Because WE ARE HUMAN BEINGS, and

Humanity has a different scope of life
From spirituality.

You can imagine…Paul wey no marry
At all and wey no get feelings, na him
Dey teach sexual morality to people
Wey dey always catch konji.

You can imagine!

These sort of religious, moral, and social
Distortions, is what makes people feel it's
Better committing suicide than continuing
Living in a world of continuous struggle and
Future sins.

Where they'll never stop feeling condemned
About their acts of masturbation or fornication,
Homosexuality, lesbianism, bisexuality, etcetera.

It's rare to find a teenager opening up to
You about the deepest pains or secrets
Of their lives; so when you find anyone
Ready to give you "their secret", the best
You can do is making them know they are

Free to talk to you about anything, that you
Love them, and that you support them so
Much.

And if your teen doesn't feel comfortable
Talking with you, suggest a more neutral
Person that he or she can find comfortable
Talking to.

[You may not even be able to suggest,
Because they would have found a way.]

It's funny when teenagers go through
Depression and adults keep wondering
"What are they thinking of that they
Are depressed?"

Some parents are even reluctant to ask
Teens if they have been thinking about
Suicide or hurting themselves.

Some fear that by asking, they will plant
The idea of suicide in their teen's head.

It's always a good idea to ask, even

Though doing so can be difficult.

Sometimes, it helps to explain why you're asking.

And one thing we ought to have understood
By now is that these guys aren't "just teenagers",
They are humans – people with emotions – and
They ought to be treated as such.

How?

With love, respect, and happiness;
Not *"they are stubborn, "they are*
Rebellious", "they are omo kekere",
And all other forms of degrading
Words we use on them.

Teens need reassurance that they are
Loved and appreciated. To treat them
As little children instead of a growing
And maturing member of the society
Can be very frustrating and annoying.

[Same way elderly-adults would be
Addressing university-youths as

Children. Like what the fuck!]

It's important to realize that if teens
Are ignored when seeking attention,
It may increase the chances of them
Harming themselves.

Leaving you with the worst possible
Outcome.

(We all know what the Sorosoke
Generation did with the #endsars
Protest.)

I was once talking to a teenager who
Was deeply frustrated about his life
And just wanted to end things.

I said these things to him:

"Give yourself two years, and you're
Already in the university. Would you
Want to kill yourself now when you
Know in two years' time you'll be free
From secondary school wahala?

"That's supposed to be the motivation
For staying alive.

"Then when the two years come, you
Give yourself another motivation for
Another (maybe) two years plan.

"Because there'll be another problem.

"There's no end to problems or depression
In this life. We only live with the ones we
Can live with, and die with the ones we
Can't live without."

Only for his response to give me
Something to also think about:

"…at the same time, I can think
That in that two years' time, will
I be doing what I want to be doing?

"Will I be living how I want to be
Living? Will my need for a drug
Keep me alive or cause an
Overdose?

"That can be a motivation

For me to also leave now."

Expressions:
Dearest Suicide

Part 13: Nothing Much

5 April 2018 2.18am
Nothing Much

I'll start from the messages you
Sent after the call, especially the
One where you said you'd not
Call back.

My silence is for the best. When I'm
Angry, I use words I mostly end up
Wishing I didn't use. And I tried not
To say anything I'd regret.

I received 60 messages from you after-
Wards; and although you had mentioned
It during the calls, my head was blown to
Pieces.

I wanted to say so many things, but
Instead, I sang a song and updated
My status.

From the start, we had a whole
Lot of free time and we were
Almost always on the phone.

I used to call you at intervals — my
Thing. You didn't say nothing about
It.

The first time anyone suggested a
Reduction in calls, I was the one.

And I was considering cost.

You sounded like I was looking
For a way to stop talking to you,
And I decided against it.

I kept calling.

You used to joke about my veins
Popping out; and though I didn't
Find it funny, I did not know — as
I now do - that you were actually
Disgusted by it.

When we started dating, I didn't
Bring up the issue of reducing call
Time, because I felt it was too early
To start sounding like I wanted to

Avoid you.

Then, I got a job - and oh! How I
Feel so sorry that I was ignorant
Of bothering you: I should have
Taken a couple of cues.

But damn!

I'm sorry.

In two months, I have only tried to
Ensure we were communicating,
But my ways are definitely not
Your ways.

And you claimed to love me,
But didn't say anything about
It.

Now, you throw words around without
Caution because you don't want a tail
On you in NYSC camp and beyond.

Wawwu! Thank God I now know. Because

The usual me would actually think I'm being
Nice when I'm calling to check on you.

But it won't happen (again). So, keep calm!

You said, you're not scared of me.
I can't remember a time when I
Stopped you from talking or
Saying your mind.

There are a few things I'd have loved
To address, but common sense is
Telling me to avoid a war of
Words.

Addressing me as "this girl" is making
My stomach turn. This girl? Okay!
Some parts of your messages are
An eye opener; and vexed as I am,
I am grateful for them.

PS. I wasn't planning to send you a
Vex-mail or a nag-mail because I was
Mad at you. I wanted to send you a
Mail, but other things happening

Around me would have contributed
To the outcome of the mail.

And that was why I wanted to talk.

Right from before we started dating, I
Took note of everything you said about
Growing up, and decided I was never
Going to use words on you in a way
That you feel like a child being scolded
For everything.

All my life, one thing I battle with is
Words, I always insist that words
Are carefully chosen with me.

Thanks for being highly insensitive.

I'd be fine.

I don't have any reason to call you
For now, plus I'm slightly vexed.

And while I get over myself, I'd like
You to have a great time in camp.

Free of any disturbance from me.

I don't intend to do anything wicked
To you. You can be rest assured.

Don't even send that kind of message
Again. What could I possibly do to you?

I've got asses to kick and a lot to
Achieve, if you don't mind, I'll like
To get busy already.

*****

And that's how the first message
Went. The first of many messages
Sent to me by my girlfriend.

And it became – maybe – the first
Of many instances where the tides
Began to turn, revealing how highly
Insensitive I had become in what
Was supposed to be a happy
Romantic relationship.

A relationship that was all the more
Opening me up on how bad I was to
Handling relationship crisis, and the
Storms that was soon to follow.

Oh, if by now you're still wondering
Where we are, we are there already.

The emails.

And you'd be seeing more of it in
Periodic chapters that'll give you
A lot of headache on the kind of
Person I am, and the problem I
Gave the one girl who (I believe)
Loved me genuinely.

And was (maybe) even ready to
Commit suicide on my matter.

Maybe.

It was the year two thousand and
Eighteen and I was in Abuja, living
With a family friend.

I had just completed my Law School year,

Been called to Bar, and decided to move

Out of my father's house for a break-free

Release from whatever pressure or problem

I knew I would be getting from home.

Having a girlfriend was what I sure wanted

And was ready to give myself into it, as I just

Couldn't cope with the thought of still not

Having a girlfriend at age twenty-five.

And now, it looked like I was transferring

The pressures and burdens of my life on

The one who wasn't even supposed to

Be a part of such burden.

So, I was off to camp and I had just

Told my girlfriend not to call me for

The periods in which I'll be in a three

Weeks NYSC Orientation camp.

Like, who fucking does that?!

Of course, me.

And more problems began
To follow.

April 19, 2018. 8.50pm
Letter to GOD (one)

Hey baby boy.

How are you? Tired and sleepy I guess.

I thank God once again for taking you
To camp safely and I'm trusting Him
To keep you safe all through.
Amen.

Actually, I know that referring to you
As GOD is fucking controversial, but
Then it's me - the one who confidently
Bears a name in a society that shrinks
At the sound and sight of it.

Thanks for loving me just as I am.
Thanks for asking me to be your
Baby girl.

Thanks for being my friend.

I'm happy I have you and I want you
To know again that I believe in you.

I'm proud of you too.

Have fun in Enugu. I'm going to
Be doing this everyday till the
Next time I see you (provided
I've got data, power on my
Phone, and good network).

I miss you so much.
I'm kissing your pictures.
I love you.

Kisses,
Baby girl.

If there was ever a time I was placed
On a ticking bomb, I think it was right
Here

And right now.

But I was too blinded by a love I wasn't
Sure I truly had, that I couldn't see the
Burden of love that was about to be
Invested by a-one who was ready to
Love me at whatever cost.

In spite of a cruel, stupid, and silly
Rule I had given.

April 20, 2018. 11.31pm
Letter to GOD (Two)

Hey baby boy,

How did your day go?

I know right? Just take care of
Yourself.

My day went well. I had a job offer, went
For the training and I left halfway into the
Whole thing, because it involved working
In a bar.

I knew ahead, plus, the company in charge
Would most likely not be paying me till June,
And what I need the cash for would be gone
By then.

Also, there's this three-weeks-tourist-guide
Job I would be applying for as soon as there
Is light and my phone comes on.

I really hope to be selected. It involves a
Whole lot of travelling and the yet-to-be-
Disclosed pay seems promising for a Lazy
Nigerian Youth.

That's that about my day.

So, I made my hair yesterday (sent you
A picture already). I forgot to mention
In yesterday's mail (well, I do not really
Like how it was done).

I look totally different, the pretty
Kinda different though.

I miss you.

Although I was sleeping when you
Called last night, I was excited to
Hear your voice.

BTW, I saw your WhatsApp status
Earlier, seemed like someone pissed
You off.

Mabinu sho gbo? Don't
Let anybody get to you.

I love you.

Take very good care of yourself, keep
Your valuables safe, watch what you
Eat and drink, and just be good.

Kisses
Baby girl.

The messages kept on coming like this
Every single day, but I couldn't think of
The best of avenues to get on with my
Life and control a situation that was

Already going out of my hand.

A love that was already going
Completely one sided.

I think I wasn't in love again. I think
I wasn't looking for anyone to be
Loved by or to love me again.

I was angry because of the way and
Manner in which I left Abuja. I was
Mad-angry, and I just didn't want
To talk to anyone about it.

Especially not my girlfriend, because I didn't
Want to sound like I was complaining about
What I really wanted to be angry and talk
About.

So, in those times and periods and moments,
And everything, I didn't want to talk to anyone
About it, so as not to wrongly blame anyone for
Something I knew I wasn't to be blamed for.

Though I was blamed for it.

I just wanted to be on my own, by myself:
Sulking up the three weeks camp in silence
And solitude.

I just wanted to bottle up, sulk
Down, and keep things in.

It was a period I so knew I wasn't going
To be able to enjoy, because I wasn't a
Sociable person by any given standard
To start with.

Things had been going on in my head
Regarding the impulse of my feelings;
And while I was angry with how things
Were going within me, there was no
Place I could transfer the anger to.

And, regrettably, it was my girlfriend
Bearing the brunt and pains…in a
Way I couldn't help against it.

April 21, 2018. 10.01pm
Letter to GOD (Three)

Hey baby boy,

How are you today? Congratulations
On being sworn in as a member of
Your NYSC Court.

Baby girl is proud of you!

So, my phone didn't come on until
Late this afternoon (no light) and
I was technically unable to send
My (job) application early enough.

Although I eventually did, I am
Yet to get a response. But I'm
Still hoping.

Meanwhile, another job popped up
(Honestly, I don't know why Buhari
Called us lazy, because I am not;
And many people aren't also).
This new job involves writing news
Articles daily for a website like that.

Starts in May.

I am really hoping to get something
To do before the month ends, so I can
Pay school fees and get this school
Thing moving.

Anyhow, how are you again? You
See, I can't keep all of these gists
Till we see.

So, without "bothering you" with
Calls or disturbing you from having
The time of your life, I'll just stick
To doing this.

BTW, what platoon were you
Sorted into? I'll found out later.

Alright, I got to go now. Till
Tomorrow again. Take very
Good care of yourself. I love
You.

Kisses
Baby girl

Expressions:

Dearest Suicide

Part 14: Organized Chaos

At a time when suicide has naturally been
Taking people away in the world all over,
The matters and issues of the coronavirus
Only made matters look more complicated
For humans.

So much so that it became easy to
Conclude (now than ever before)
That the world needed to end fast
So that life can begin all over again.

More like, make everything just crash
And end so that whoever create this
World in the first place go just click
The damn refresh button or restart.

So that we can start life all over again.

From scratch.

Clean slate. No Covid or Buhari anywhere.

When the SARS outbreak occurred back
Then in the year two thousand and three,
And the Bird Flu that broke out two years

After that, there was a surge in the rates
Of suicide amongst older youths and adults.

Due to the fear of what was to
Happen or befall humanity.

People became overwhelmed with
Fear and anxiety, that we all were
Scared to even breeeet.

Coz we learnt it's an airborne disease.

With 2020, things only got worse for
Us humanity on a scale never before
Experienced by anyone (still) living.

First of all, it was supposed to be a
Health crisis typical to a relatively
Unknown Wuhan.

This crisis was thought to be a common
China situation – since they are always
Known for creating these sort of flus
And diseases in the first place.

Eating fried bats, grilled frogs, roasted
Lizard and every nonsense thing they
Can think of.

So we just thought it was a normal
Disease for them, and that after a
While, they would be fine.

Only for us to start hearing of how the
Disease was astronomically spreading
Across oceans and atlantics.

In a surprising and bewildering manner.

With millions of people in several
Continents of the world restricted
To their respective homes, due to
What was now called a pandemic.

E kon be like sey rapture wan
Finally happun.

Even churches, mosques, the market,
Economy, and sports as a whole (with
Football in particular) put to a halt for

Several months.

Hence, the global shutdown.

And with many losing their jobs in the
Process, there was a constant worry
About what could become a high,
Uncalculated and unexpected
Rise in the rates of suicides.

Similar to what was happening
During the SARS and Flu seasons.

The global stats might have felt like a
Figure-padded and slightly exaggerated
Stuff, to pass a political statement and
An economic theory between the USA
And China.

In the struggle for who becomes
The next World Power.

But facts remained that millions of
People died all over the world, and
Millions of people lost their jobs,

Since the start of the "China virus".

As Donald Trump preferred to call it.

With social distancing came an increase in
Social isolation, resulting in a high level of
Loneliness for lots and lots of people who
Had previously been struggling to have a
Life prior to the pandemic.

Add this psychological trauma to the fear
Of contracting the disease, and you have
A high level of hopelessness and spiraling
Thoughts in the minds of the average human.

In Nigeria for example, there were issues
Of government palliatives that were only
Meant for a category politically regarded
As "poorest of the poor".

A category for which we'll never get to
Know the exact people over five billion
Naira was spent on to cushion the effect
Of what hunger was doing to the people.

Of course, this led to human violence
In some states where the pandemic
Was hitting hard, due to the lockdown.

Or do we want to say we didn't hear of
The different cases of communal clashes
And street robbery in states like Lagos
And Ogun?

Let's not even go to the story of how
Different palliative warehouses were
Looted by hungry youths (maybe the
Angry ones), all because government
Decided to store (and allow to spoil)
What was supposed to be shared.

And talking about the social distancing
And self-isolation in itself, introverts like
Myself had been on the social-distancing
And self-isolation for as long as we could
Possibly remember.

Long before the word "lockdown"
Ever became common knowledge.

Such that, when the new system became
Official, we felt sort of endangered by the
Development of the seat-at-home rule.

Coz our private lives and inner spaces
Became threatened by noisy extroverts
Who couldn't understand what it meant
To shut the fuck up for just an hour.

And for the motivational talkers and
Their noise about learning a new skill,
It began raising huge question marks
On certain adverts we had been seeing
Online prior to the lockdown.

"How to earn 300 dollars working from home".

Oh yeah, with everyone now sitting
Our asses at home: where the fuck
Was the 300 dollars we were all to
Start earning from our homes?

Y'all are welcome.

On the flip side, a lot of bank accounts

Were trekking on the streets of twitter,
All because one celebrity decided to do
Corona-giveaway.

For average broke ass niggas.

You'll go there, drop your account number
Out of a feeling of *"God no go shame us o,*
What if luck shine on me?"

Then you'll now be in a *"Omooo!"* level,
Wondering who-are-the-those showing
Proofs of bank transfers, when shingbai
Is not coming to your side!

If that's not a suicidal feeling,
Should we just call it village
People?

Sapa x 30BG equals what??

Well, the suicidal effect of the virus
In itself already claimed its first major
Victim in the German State of Hesse's
Finance Minister, Thomas Schäfer.

In a note he left behind, Thomas explained
That he was deeply concerned that he would
Not be able to fulfil the population's huge
Expectations and demands for financial aid.

He was a politician. Maybe a technocrat.
But he was definitely a political leader.

And because he felt he wouldn't be able to
Handle the demands and responsibilities
That came with governing the people at
Such a critical state, he thought it best to
Kill himself.

Rather than just jejely step down and
Resign and peacefully go home to be
With his family.
E still dey hard me to understand the matter.

Also, Jo'Vianni Smith, a fifteen-year-old
Teenager was found dead at her home
In California, USA.

Jo'Vianni was still in high school and
Was very much active on social media

When she deemed it fit to take her
Life.

Not leaving any goodbye-note behind,
Her mom believed she was stressed
And overwhelmed by her inability to
Cope with the coronavirus lockdown.

Similar to the story of Jo'Vianni Smith
Is the case of another fifteen-year-old
Boy who took his life.

Just because he was feeling isolated from
The world after the announcement of the
Lockdown.

His mood changed in the space of a few
Days, and he kept saying he couldn't wait
For it to be over and that he wanted to
"Fast forward it all."

This one happened in UK.

There's also the moving story of a
Man who killed his entire family

And himself during this same
Lockdown.

Parents of the man (who was said
To be a builder), were completely
Devastated by the incident.

The grieving mom had this to say
Concerning the situation:

*"I felt that I was doing all that I
Could as a parent to leave the
Communication open.*

*"Sometimes we may need to stop
And worry about the kids that we
Don't think we need to worry
About."*

Apart from the issues of loneliness and
Boredom that came with the lockdown,
One other thing that personally drained
Me during these times was job search.

The search for a job.

I've often always wondered why at
My age, I still don't know how to get
A means of knowing or learning how
To work.

That's the truth. That's the basic
Truth, and there's no other truth
Other than that.

I don't have a job, I don't have a source
Of income, and I don't have anything
I'm doing that can give me money.

Well, I can't start apportioning any
Thread of blames on anyone for now,
Even though I have a ready-made name
That'll spill itself in the course of my talk.

But all I know is that prior to when corona
Happened, I'd never been able to learn how
To work, know how to work, or even carryout
Any form of business trade whatsoever.

Let me expressly say that I was never
Taught how to think of how to get a

Job or how to make money or how
To earn for a living.

The only thing I had in my head up until
The end of my University education was
That *"when you graduate, you will get a
Job in a company that'll be paying you
Well"*.

Maybe they don't teach it. Maybe life
Makes you learn it yourself. So, it's safe
To say I've never had the opportunity of
Earning a salary in my life before.

The first ever time I found myself
"Going to work" was during my
Law school externship.

Didn't have any work or experience
Before then.

And even at that, I got bored of it
So quickly that I could only manage
To go there six times in the six
Weeks of the externship.

Coz I wasn't doing anything there,
And those who came were reading
For Bar Finals – aside gisting, eating,
And sleeping.

And I just had this feeling that they
Were all better than me and more
Experienced in 'the practice of law'
Than I was/am.

Yes, there have always been this sort
Of disappointment that always made
Me feel like *"my friends know this and
That, and are working at so and so."*

That knowledge and the sour feeling
That always came with it never gave
Me peace of mind at all.

That knowledge always made me
Feel like a useless person that'll
Never find a place to call my own
Job, or office, or work.

Add that it was kinda clear that I didn't

Know book, based on what was shown
On my certificate, so it didn't even make
Me in anyway get excited in dropping my
CV anywhere or submitting it to any firm
As opposed to the beautiful ideas I had in
My head.

Coz I concluded within myself that I
Wouldn't be able to meet up with
The expectations or qualification
Requirements of any firm.

Like someone once said, being born
In Nigeria is a disadvantage: life is
Automatically leading you 1-0.

Then being born to a poor or middle
Class family, you're already two goals
Down.

And if you now happen to be the
First born, Life 3 – 0 You.

There's no other way to say it
Better than that.

I'm a home boy. I'm home grown.
I don't go out. And I don't even
Have the desire to go out.

Even if I want to.

Because I'll always feel weak and want
To drag myself back to my room – coz
Of how disconnected I'll feel whenever
I'm outside the house.

Saying these sort of things sef makes
One sound like an unserious person,
As though there's no other person
In the world going through these
Sort of difficulties.

Even though they prefer keeping
Quiet about it and making people
Feeling like they are doing well or
That they have hammer.

It was this exact difficulty I was going
Through in the few months I spent in
Abuja after I was Called to Bar.

Because of my desire to seek out ways in
Solving my problems and pushing myself
Beyond limits, I chose to go live in Abuja
(With my family friends) for a while.

Whether it was going to be for a short
While or a long while, all I knew was
That I just wanted to leave the house
And find myself.

Coz it looked like something impossible
For me to do – to just wake up one day
And say I want to leave the house in a
Search for greener pastures.

I was looking for a way to push myself
Out of my 'comfort zone' when it felt
Like I wasn't useful to anyone at home
Again.

I'd already missed out on NYSC in
October 2017 because I couldn't
Find my name in the Senate list
On the NYSC portal.

An error that was done by my
School, for removing the first
Zero in my matric number.

Inputting 9085506,
Instead of 09085506.

So in a bid not to sit down at home
Again and start thinking of my life
All over again (after all the different
Delays and sitting at home in the
Past), I chose to go to Abuja instead.

The hidden line in the mix there was
That I just wanted to run away from
The house and find for myself a life
Outside the house boy I'm used to.

An environment that didn't have to do
With Daddy and Mommy and Parents
And Problems and Responsibilities and
Accusations and everything that makes
Me feel more of a useless person than
The first-born-child mentality my dad
Wanted to 'stupidly' put into my head.

Right there in the house, I wasn't learning
Anything and wasn't getting anywhere.

The exposures I was finding my colleagues
Swimming in just wasn't open to me so long
As I continued staying in that house.

I was angry with myself and angry
With the disadvantaged life I was
Living in.

To be fair to myself and my conscience,
My dad didn't do well in making me feel
Like a happy child or person: it was always
One accusation and scolding and rebuke
After another.

I totally lost every ounce of confidence
Life gives human by default.

And with the way he was advancing in his
Career and helping every other person get
A job, I was honestly expecting him to do
A lot in terms of helping me get a job.

At least, that would have covered
Up for all his 'bad deeds' in my life.

After all, the ones who claim to be
Up and doing in their career always
Help their children get a job.

All the Pastors. All the Big Men.
All the Politicians. All the big time
Fathers. Every single one of them.

That's what I believed. That's what I thought.

But the more I thought about it, the more
I realized I was in a world of my own, and
My dad wasn't going to help me get a job.

Aside just sitting at home and opening
The gate for him, and being blamed for
The rats doing Olympics in the kitchen.

And the more frustrated I was about
Trying to think things through for me,
The more I needed to take permission
From him before I go anywhere.

While still being in his house.

I couldn't even be bold enough to ask
Any friend to come see me in at home,
Because of the sort of fear I had within
Me that something would go wrong
Somewhere.

It's not even as if I was brought up that
Way in the first place: to be going friends
Visiting or having friends come visit me.

So, whether it was an act of being like
The rebellious (and later proverbial
Prodigal son) or just me looking for
A way to get my life working, Abuja
Was the next destination for me
In January twenty-eighteen.

But this still didn't mean I wasn't sad.

I was angry each time they called me
A lawyer, when I couldn't even boast
Of a certificate that would get me the
Job of a lawyer in a law firm.

And being that I also didn't know how
To "hustle", I was living off that hands
Of every other person that was working
Around me there.

It was angrying me, it was annoying
Me, it was sadding me, it was vexing
Me.

I wished I could shout, but I couldn't
Find my voice. I wished I could talk,
But I couldn't find the words.

I wished I could cry, but I couldn't
Find my tears. I wished I could fight,
But I didn't even have the strength.

It was always depressing having to
Go to a restaurant where life was
Bubbling for every other person
But me.

Because every other person there had one
Thing or the other to contribute towards
The growth of the place (in terms of skills,

Logistics, and calculation of money.)

And me? Nothing!

I just couldn't find my place there,
No matter how bad I tried, neither
Could I even find what I could do to
Serve as my contribution towards
The success of the restaurant.

Aside eating free food.

Knowing I didn't have money
To (at least) buy my own food.

Knowing I didn't have a job.

I knew I was depressed about it,
But I doubted if anyone ever got
To notice it.

Coz I think I was good at masking
My sadness with shrewd silence.

And what I even wished I could add

To the place wasn't happening for
Me, coz it felt more like I was a
Fish unable to climb tree.

A small boy placed in a small box.

Maybe it was a big box. Maybe it was
Even bigger, but I was finding myself
Frustrated by not being able to fix
My life on the job front.

So, when job employment wasn't
Coming through, I wasn't ready to
Ridicule my life any further, under
Anyone.

I said I was going to allow my pen
And lifestyle do the job and work
For me.

That's how I turned my Expressions
Into my fulltime job – trying to create
Words and stories from my personal
Life that can make sense to someone
Out there.

Even if it meant giving you words
You wouldn't want to reason with.

And I wasn't chasing after the crowd
At all, I just wanted one audience.

One person that can read my
Expressions and find life in it.

I believed if I could find one person
And just get as little as one like, the
Rest would sort it self in the long run.

No matter how long the run is.

I didn't even know what to call myself:
Whether a founder, bricklayer, CEO, or
Whatever; I just knew I had given my-
Self a job, and I had become my own
Boss.

Whatever it was, I knew I was going
To become a writing legend in no
Distant future.

But all the same, I was still physically
Fed up and mentally exhausted about
The idea of not still being able to get
A job.

So after NYSC and still finding myself
Sitting down at home, I decided to
Ask my friend certain questions.

I knew him to be someone who had
Been working right from his secondary
School or so, and even witnessed his
Working abilities first hand, while at
The University together.

So I asked him some questions…

At what age did you enter university?

Oluwapelumi Awotedu: Twenty-one.

Why was it so? What happened?
Money.

We didn't have money for me to have

Begun tertiary education earlier, so I
Had to wait unintentionally.

Was there any benefit it added
To you?

Yes.

There was this confidence I never
Enjoyed during my primary and
Secondary education because I
Was so young.

I enjoyed that boldness (at the
University), and lived the best
I could.

I was myself.

Were you a full time or part-time
Student? And why?

Part-time.

Did both entrance exam. Gained

Admission into both. Lost full time
Admission. Resorted to Part-time.

Who was sponsoring your education?
And how were you seeing or getting
A job to do?

I sponsored it.

Dad already left an aspect of his
Job for me to handle. I used the
Proceeds to fend for my total
Upkeep and education.

There was a ready market for jobs.

What made you lose the
Fulltime admission?

I did direct entry. So the diploma result
I was using wasn't accepted. I was told
It's professional, not academics.

"Dad already left an aspect of his job
For me to handle. I used the proceeds to

110

Fend for my total upkeep and education."

This is even the main reason why I asked
All these questions, because I don't know
How to work, and I thought my dad would
Give me something to start with.

I was reading a book (about temperament
Though), and got to a part and started to
Think away, then I thought of asking you
Some questions about jobs, money, and
Working.

I wanted to learn something from it,
Because I've always been frustrated
By it.

Yes, I was always reporting to him when
I was at home and just gained admission,
But he later said I should be keeping the
Proceeds.

So in a way, you got trained in it too
By your dad?

Yes.

Don't know if I've found what I'm
Looking for, but I'm grateful for
Your answers.

The fending part, I guess, is what
One finds out or discovers himself
Abi?

If fortunate.

I was.

If one gets help, it's very fine.

In my own case, I've never learnt
How to fend for myself. I'm still
Learning the 'how' on my own.

No one taught me. If I can leave this
House like Arya (Game of Thrones),
It would have been good.

I hope you understand what I'm saying,

**I'm talking about what I wished I could
Have, not complaining about what I
Don't have.**

*The one thing you need most is money.
Money comes through a source.*

Do you have any source of income presently?

No.

**Sebi it's a vocational job or paid job
That they call source of income, aside
Assets and all?**

Yes. You need that first.

**That's the one that's giving me
Problems. But I'm grateful with
Your answers.**

Thank you for thanking me.

You know, I was already approaching 28;
And being the first born child of my family,

It felt very much embarrassing that I still
Couldn't figure out how to fend for myself.

Without getting the help of my parents.

More than the fact that it was embarrassing
To be asking for stuff like transport money,
Money for data, airtime, and money to go
Out, I couldn't even boast of any money I
Could call my own.

Either way I wanted to put it, whether
Going by way of motivational speakers
Or trying to look out for a positive hope
To bring out of my situation, the only
Thing I could possibly pin down was that,
It's my dad who didn't train me to know
How to work or get a job.

No blames. Just choosing to
Conveniently look at it from
That angle.

Na him cause am.

All he was only talking about was my
Books, and I became so fed up of books
That I was repeatedly failing my books.

Until I finished with third-class.

Yeah, I couldn't say this out before, coz
Each time I thought of it, I would want
To ignore the situation and say *"what*
About those who don't have a dad, yet
Their working?"

Then I would answer myself by saying:
"Well, maybe me too, I shouldn't have
Had a dad, so that I'll be able to have
A job or work at an early age".

Different strokes for different folks huh?

Let's just call it organized chaos.

Expressions:
Dearest Suicide

Part 15: E-mails

April 22, 2018. 2.58pm
Letter to GOD (Four)

Hey baby boy,

I actually find it interesting that
I've been doing this for four days,
And you have no idea (I believe so).

So, how are you? Church was great,
Sermon was about the 21st century
Evangelism.

Many things on my mind again; but
One of the sweetest things I heard
Was "Gideon - mighty man of valor".

It made me think of you. And that's
One of the reasons why I referred to
You as "superman" earlier.

I should read Judges sef.

There's no response yet from the
Tour Guide job I applied for. If by

The end of today there's no news,
I'll forget it.

Lest I forget, why did you say my
"Love intoxication" is getting
Aggressive?

I didn't understand,
Make me understand.

I see you're having a good time already;
I wish you more wonderful moments
That would eventually be beautiful
Memories when you look back on
Them.

PS: I might send another mail at
Night, like part two of day four.

Take very good care of yourself.
I miss you and I love you.

Kisses
Baby girl

Could it ever have been possible
That "this girl" was 'just bugging
Me'?

Or was I the one clearly blind to the
Deep love and feelings from a girl so
Unrestrictive of herself, feelings, and
Emotions that she was still talking to
Me despite what I'd told her?

Something was really wrong somewhere.
Something I didn't know. And something
That I so knew would be revealed soonest.

April 23, 2018. 6.18pm
Letter to GOD (Five)

Hey baby boy,

How are you? I got the pictures you
Sent. Wait! Were you trying to do the
Shaku-shaku dance at some point?

Okay, I must say that comme d'habitude

(As usual) you look dashing in those
Pictures, but I am not dashing you out.

Damn! You're so cute!

Since it's Monday sef, just allow me
To crush on you all over again.

Baby, why so fine nah?

Pour moi, it's been a very long and
Short day, no light at all. The whole
Place is just somehow.

Boring and annoying-how.

The day seemed unending initially
But now it's past six, and I've only
Been able to do almost nothing.

I've finally accepted that the tourist
Job isn't coming, c'est la vie (such is
Life). But the other news thingy is
Promising, as I have been added
To their WhatsApp group.

Gideon, have fun, I already told you
I won't disturb you and I'm doing all
I can to stick to my promise.

Well, you're doing a good job
At keeping up too.

Thank you!

Take very good care of yourself.
I miss you and I love you.

P.S. If I'm not wrong, you're
In platoon one abi?

P.S.S. I'm trying to imagine the look
On your face when you eventually
Find these mails.

Kisses
Baby girl.

Five days gone already, and I still
Didn't know she had been sending
Me emails.

Every day, for the past five days!

I had only tried to give her some
Phone calls, and she still tried her
Best not to say anything about it
During the calls, despite the fact
That it was surely itching her to
Say.

It's easier to kill a man through
Sex or food….right?

But how about through emails?

April 23, 2018. 6.29pm
Letter to GOD (Six)

Hey baby boy,
I've got a cold.

I feel sick. But, I'll be fine.

You know nah.

How are you today? For me,
Asides the cold, I kinda feel
Down.

I could link it up with many things,
But I am really trying to keep my
Head above the water.

I miss you.

I know how important this time
Is, but honestly, I really wish we
Were together.

Anywhere on earth, just the two of us.

I want to hear your voice without the
Interference of a phone, see your face
And be able to touch it.

I want to be lost in your embrace.

I just want to hear you say that
We'd be fine, we'll always be
Together and we'd always

Make us work.

I miss you.

There's so many things I want to say
To you, but first, I want to know the
Taste of your lips. I want to sing my
Heart out with you backing me up.

I want to see you, play with you, read
With you, pray with you and above all,
Disturb you every chance I get.

I thought it was gonna take long
Before I breakdown from missing
You; but damn!, I am not so strong
Afterall.

And, as all of me longs for you,
I patiently look forward to seeing
You again.

Because for now, that is
All I can do.

Let me just focus on maximizing this
"Somewhat" free time, although you're
Stuck on my mind with a couple of things.

I love you and I am missing you.

The koko of this mail is that I miss
You.

Kisses,
Baby girl

April 25, 2018. 10.23pm
Letter to GOD (Seven)

Hey baby boy,

How are you today? Well, I
Woke up to your "text".

And though twas just two words,
I couldn't stop smiling till I opened
Your Whatsapp message.

"Nope!".

I can't even lie, I was pained.

I missed you the whole of yesterday,
Resisted the temptation to call you
At different times.

And instead, I asked for a kiss
(Comman kiss me) and you
Said nope!

I wasn't expecting you to come
Kiss me, and I wasn't expecting
A nope either!

Guess, I raised my hopes too high.

There's no way you kuku could have
Known how bad I was missing you
Yesterday (till you find these mails).

But I let it go sha.

I got over myself eventually,

And it feels good to.

About my day, went out to pickup
Some stuff that was ordered from
The mobile billboard and I got back
Quite tired, so, I took a nap.

Then, I was having a conversation
With a friend and I mentioned how
You like saying either "that's your
Problem" or "that's not my problem".

And just laidat, he said he had idea
For a song and he's going to use the
"That's your problem" thing as chorus.

I'm kinda getting tired of dropping you
These mails; but then, it's almost like
The only connection I have with you
Presently.

So I'm just going to continue.

I have asked myself severally, "what if
He finally gets the mails and gets upset

Because they are too many?

"What if he doesn't buy the idea of
You sending him many messages?

"What if? What if? What if?"
But I can't kill myself.

We don't talk anymore because of
"NYSC", and I don't know when
We'd get back to talking.

I can't wait till then to reach out to you.

I have never been scared of reaching
Out to you except now that I have to
Think twice before calling you, even
If it's just once.

I just hope you remember that I'm
Treating you as you want, so that
You can be happy?

But I don't like it.

I love you, and I mean it every time.
Have fun, and make sure you take
Very good care of yourself.

I miss you. But, this time I'm
Regulating it. Healthier that
Way!

Kisses,
Baby girl

Hmmmmm!

"I just hope you remember that I'm
Treating you as you want, so that
You can be happy?"

if I were to be prosecuted for these
Actions of mine, how many years
Would have been my jail term?

I mean, a girl going to all lengths and
Going through all pains to write me
These degrees of emotional emails,
Yet I couldn't see it for one stupid

Reason of mine.

What ever happened to even
Checking up my mails sef?

Did you ever notice the time she
Was sending the mails? Some of
Them were at midnight!

Mid-fucking-night!

I wished I could reply to these mails
As they came in. I really wished.

But the best I can do is allow you
Read all of 'em the more.

All of the tales that could have
Made someone else – someone
Else not strong enough – to give
Up.

To give up on life.

But she never stopped.

She never stopped.

She kept on writing….

April 26, 2018. 10.12am
Letter to GOD (Eight)

Hey baby boy,

How are you today?

Well, I am fine!

Everything I might want to say today
Has been said by Nathan Skyes and
Ariana Grande in their song "Over
And Over Again."

Enjoy the lyrics.

From the way you smile to the
Way you look, you capture me
Unlike no other.

'From the first hello, yeah, that's
All it took. And suddenly, we had
Each other.

'And I won't leave you.
Always be true.

'One plus one, two for life.
Over and over again.

'So, don't ever think I need more
I've got the one to live for. No one
Else will do, and I'm telling you.

'Just put your heart in my hands.

'Promise it won't get broken. We'll
Never forget this moment. Yeah,
We'll stay brand-new, cause I'll
Love you over and over again.

'Over and over again

'From the heat of night to the
Break of day I'll keep you safe

And hold you forever and the
Sparks will fly, they will never
Fade.

'Cause every day gets better
And better.

'And I won't leave you.
Always be true.

'One plus one, two for life
Over and over again.

'So, don't ever think I need more
I've got the one to live for. No one
Else will do, and I'm telling you.

'Just put your heart in my hands.

'Promise it won't get broken. We'll
Never forget this moment. Yeah,
We'll stay brand-new, cause I'll
Love you over and over again.

'Over and over again.

'Boy, when I'm with you I lose track
Of time. When I'm without you you're
Stuck on my mind.

'Be all you need till the day that I
Die, I'll love you over and over
Again.

'So, don't ever think I need more
I've got the one to live for. No one
Else will do, and I'm telling you.

Just put your heart in my hands.

'Promise it won't get broken. We'll
Never forget this moment. Yeah,
We'll stay brand-new, cause I'll
Love you over and over again.

'Yeah, over and over again.

'Over and over again.'

Kisses,
Baby girl.

April 26, 2018. 2.46pm
Letter to GOD (8.2)

Hey baby boy,

I am not happy (don't get yourself
Worked up) I'll be fine eventually
(I know).

You can reassure me though.

Sadly, I can't even pray about my
Unhappiness (I'm that wrecked).

It feels like all my attempts at
Breaking free from this spot I've
Been stuck on for a while now is
Just taking me round in circles.

Is this what trusting God solely
Feels like? Because nothing
Makes sense to me right
Now.

I know I'm going to make it

Eventually, but all I see right
Now is a mess.

You sure know I know about this
Phase of being like a seed buried
In the earth, receiving nutrients
For the time when it would blossom.

I'm just saying it feels like the
Blossoming isn't forthcoming.

I think I need your help with Bible
Refs right now as per you're the
Bible scholar I am proud to have.

Baby, I feel like I'm losing my mind
Worrying over stuff, but I swear I
Can't stop myself from worrying.

I've been quite moody/aggressive
That I don't even know what is
Getting me angry.

Been trynna read but I can't make
Sense of my books.

There's been too much in the head
To make the books sink. I've been
So cranky, I think I need me some
Sex in my life.

But celibacy be laughing at me like...

Really, mo ti miss e gan.

I already knew I'd send more than
One mail today. How could I have
Said everything at 10am?

I miss your wahala biko, I can't
Even deny! But you be fronting
Like you dunn miss me.

Serious sombori, my future
Money-focused-minded
Sweetheart.

Yinmu.

When you're ready, goann carry
Your formal chats in my message

Box. I don't know the guy that's
Been sending me those messages.

I want my baby boy.

Anyhow sha, I can't believe
I smiled at some points.

Awwwwn…your love be boosting my morale!

I love you so much…you can read
The previous mail again.

How do I make you see this without
Telling you to check? Hmmmm.

Oya, bye bye.

Kisses,
Baby girl.

[Silence…]

Expressions:
Dearest Suicide

Part 16: Many Money Problems

In December twenty-sixteen, I was
Talking with a Law School mate about
My desire to join a then-popular ponzi
Scheme where people cashed out within
Days of investing.

MMM.

I'd been hearing about it for a
While and how some people I
Know of were cashing out in
Their thousands of naira.

Even millions.

On the day I planned joining with
My last 10k, MMM crashed!

Isn't the Lord good?

I was told about MMM on Friday; I had
Fifteen kay in my account, with a plan
To use ten kay for the 'investment',
While keeping the remaining five
Thousand naira to myself.

To keep body and soul together,
Pending when my money returns.

I was told I'll get fifty thousand
Naira in returns!

I even heard the Pastor preaching
Against MMM in Church on Sunday,
Giving us a theological interpretation
Of MMM as 'Making Many Mad.'

He explained that it was a form of
Madness and sheer laziness for an
Average Nigerian youth to believe
He can put his money into a scheme
And get double the amount without
Doing anything.

That it meant robbing Peter to pay Paul.

Well, I needed my money; so in my
Mind, I said he was just saying his
Own.

No time!

My plan was that first thing on
Monday morning, I would tell
My friend to register for me,
So I get my share before the
System begins to hang.

She was my direct seat partner in a
Row of seats at the auditorium-like
Lagos Law School Campus.

I hadn't even seen her on Monday
Morning when news filtered across
The auditorium…….that MMM had
Crashed.

I didn't know how I would have felt if
I'd dropped my cash before the crash,
But I knew those who put in one million
Naira or borrowing thousands of naira
To cash out with, would have been hit
Hard by the crash.

A lot would have been suicidal:
Definitely, more definitely, and
Most-most definitely.

My friend also had her money stuck.

It was her third time though, so she
Had already made enough money
Not to be worried by the loss.

And you know, right from my
University days, I'd always seen
The ponzi scheme of a thing as
Bad business.

But, due to the fact that I was now
In dire need of money, and was no
Longer under any fellowship (ponzi
Scheme was a sin in the University
Fellowship), I saw it as a good time
To get into the MMM business.

Only for the scheme to crash.

Wasn't the Lord good to me?

So I thought.

So June twenty-eighteen when I

Got out of the NYSC Camp, I was
In desperate need of a good place
I could rent self-con.

I couldn't stay another day in the
Church's corpers' lodge I found,
And NCCF was an outright no-no
For me.

Coz I had already endured that era
In the University, and I couldn't try
Enduring another episode of family
House nonsense and all its spiritual
Atrocities.

Enugu could have been said to be
Just any state in the eastern part
Of Nigeria (for we Lagosians), but
Securing an ideal accommodation
Was by no means a cheap something.

Prices were rising like Ijebu garri.

Using head knowledge, I was thinking I
Could get a place for maximum, 50k; but

On getting there, I found out that even a
House of a hundred would have to be a
Managed facility.

I didn't want a roommate, and I wasn't
Interested in sharing toilet with any
Neighbour, so I was told I would have

To look for a minimum of one hundred
And fifty thousand naira, before I can
Have a "conveniently manageable
Accommodation."

Issokay!

My parents didn't have that kind of
Money at the time, and I was getting
Frustrated by the continuous rules
Placed on us by the Church Corpers'
Excos.

I wasn't working, my PPA wasn't
Paying me, state allawee was 986
Naira, and the 19,8 from Federal
Government wasn't going to serve

Any purposeful purpose in the quest
For accommodation.

I thus had to look elsewhere for
Cash, because I couldn't bare the
Annoyance in the lodge anymore.

On a certain Tuesday like that, I kept
Staring at a WhatsApp message I saw
On a WhatsApp group, explaining how
I can double my money within twenty-
Four hours.

I'd never believed these guys. If at all
I even wanted to, the near-hit which I
Missed on MMM was enough warning
Or lesson already.

More so, I was already in the know of
Scammers everywhere and how they
Dupe people of their hard-earned cash
Online in stories that touch the kidney.

So I ignored the message and
Went about my daily dealings.

Until I saw the message again
In yet another group.

Has it ever occurred to you that the
Moment your mind starts desiring to
Do something, you easily begin to see
Things that the mind wants you to do?

More like, on a normal day, you
Wouldn't have bothered yourself
With these things o, but because
Your attention has been altered,
Everything along that line begins
To come your way.

That's how this one was doing me.

For some annoying reasons, it felt as
Though I was dumped in Enugu, coz
I didn't want to go there (after camp)
Without guarantee of accommodation.

And the 250k flat my friend saw that
Was to be divided into three people
(With me being the third person) was

Taken by someone else.

Coz I couldn't bring my own part.

Now, I thought to myself: if I do this
Thing just two times, I can get almost
Half the money I'm looking for, and I
Wouldn't have to bother my parents
About giving me any money again.

This was looking more like a
Potential opportunity than
A possible scam.

To satisfy my thinking, I copied the
Message and sent it as a DM to the
Sender, then added a last line:

"How true is this?"

Speaking good English, using my common
Sense initiative, and being open, honest,
And truthful (READ: stupidly naïve) had
Been my mantra for so long a time, so I
Was expecting an honest and truthful

Response from him.

On Wednesday, he replied me.

After few minutes of chatting, he
Advised I go for the one of fifteen
Thousand, so I can get thirty kay
Within twenty-four hours.

I was happy!

For once in my life, I found myself
'Transacting an online business',
And believing in a scheme I'd never
Previously entertained.

And within minutes of ending the
Conversation, I used my UBA app
In transferring fifteen thousand
Naira out of my nineteen kay
Allawee to him.

Along with other required details
Like my email address, my phone
Number, and the bank account I

Would like to receive my money
On.

Business is business, and I don't
Like stalling when doing business.

I didn't even know his name. All I
Knew was that I was going to be
Thirty-thousand-naira richer in
The next twenty-four hours.

I've always been a patient and
Understanding guy. Maybe too
Patient as to be a fool atimes,
So I didn't fret the following day
When I didn't see an alert on my
Phone.

My plan was that I would wait until
10am before I begin thinking about
The possibility of my being scammed.

Exactly around that time, his call
Came in. All hope was assured.

Said he had been trying to call
Me but it was switched off.

I apologized. Told him my phone
Died the night before, and I was
Just able to charge.

He then said the slot had been filled
By someone else, and I needed to
Migrate to another plan to be able
To get my money.

Eh gawd! Which kain bad market be dis?

I wasn't expecting to hear any tales
By moon light in the morning again,
Since I'd made the transfer to him
Instantly at the end of our talk the
Previous day.

I thought being timely with sending
Money meant you'll get a timely
Response?

So what plan was now available if

That was gone? He said the one of
Fifty kay to get hundred kay.

I went mad!

Fifty thousand naira keee?! How come?!!

*"What about the fifteen kay I sent
To you? What happened to it??"*

He said it's still available, but that
The slot was no longer available
Because…(he used one English to
Explain a beautiful rubbish that
Couldn't even be understood with
The way my blood was pumping
And my heart was pounding).

I tried to be calm, but I was already on fire.

Maybe I was too foolish as to try to
Have an empathetic conversation
With a professional scammer, coz
I was explaining to him how *"I am
Just a corper"*, and that it was my

Allawee I used in doing the plan.

My guy said he understood.

So what are we going to do?

"Borrow." He said I should borrow.

Wahala!!!

Who do I know that can borrow
Me fifty thousand naira in this
Buhari-Nigeria?

After making several calls, I told
Him it was only ten kay I could
Get, that he should help me add
Twenty-five from his side so that
It'll be fifty.

And I'll balance him once
I get the hundred.

I was begging this guy in front of
Skye Bank at Holy Ghost (a popular

Area in Enugu metropolis).

The calculation was so rusty on first
Thought, but my plan was to send the
Ten kay in my savings so he can add it
To the fifteen I had previously sent to
Him.

And then complete the transaction
From his end.

That was when I found out there
Was an issue on my Skye account,
And I wouldn't be able to withdraw
From it.

Fuck shiiii!

In the process of begging this guy, the
Calls were even ending abruptly, and
Bros wasn't picking my calls periodically,
Saying he was busy with other clients.

It was even someone else
That was talking to me!

That thing scared the shit out of me.

I feared I had just been scammed,
But I was prayerfully hoping I wasn't.

Prayerfully hoping ni o.

But I wasn't calm anymore.

I kept telling myself that once the deal
Was over, I would never place my hands
On such money doubling strategy again.

On Friday morning, my WhatsApp
Messages to him weren't delivering,
And I couldn't see his DP anymore.

His phone was also switched off.

It was then it dawned on me that
E DON HAPPEN!

The way this 'motor' jammed me
Was unexplainable; I was in shock.

It wasn't the case that I was stupid, but
Because I had already first sent out the
Fifteen kay without getting it back, my
Fear and desperation made me then
Transfer the additional ten kay.

I was trying to hold a reasonable conversation
With a Nigerian whom I believed would be as
Honest as I was with my explanations.

I didn't know he was a professional
Hushpuppi, using the language of
The streets for me.

I guess my 'honest sillynity' allowed me
Believe all he was saying up to the point
Where I couldn't sense he would switch
Off his phone and block me on WhatsApp.

Mumu me.

Samuel Tuesday, Guaranty Trust Bank.

That was the only details I had of a
Guy that had now gone into thin air.

Officially, I had been scammed!

[Teaaars in heaven].

Not knowing what next to do, I quickly
Sent a facebook message to UBA's Leo
So he could help me get back my twenty
Five thousand naira.

He replied that I get a court affidavit
Or a police report and take it to the
Nearest UBA branch for immediate
Action.

It was then it occurred to me that
I was an intelligent lawyer (or so I
Believed) who had just allowed
Himself to be swindled by the
Ones I once called touts.

My heart was in an emotional state
Of a disappointing disappointment.

Getting to the Police Station, I couldn't
Even confidently say where I met the

Guy from (coz even me myself knew
What the answer would be).

All I found myself saying was *"I saw his*
Message on a WhatsApp group and sent
Him a message, that's how we started
Talking."

I knew I was a fool, but I wasn't ready
To allow these officers remind me of
That again. I just wanted them to help
Me get back my money before he runs
Away.

Where do they even want to see him?
I was told to bring one thousand naira
So as to be given a police report. But I
Didn't have, so I left.

Was I expecting a Police report
To be free?

Maybe. Maybe not.

Maybe because my senses had just

Been swiped and scammed and
Destroyed.

Or maybe because I didn't have any
Other naira on me again, so I was
Expecting to get every possible
Help I could get.

FROM POLICE OFFICERS. Okay!

That was on a Saturday.

I walked back to the lodge under
The rain, with hunger in my belly
And no person to tell what just
Happened.

"PaGidi! Odindin lawyer!
Scammed on WhatsApp!"

Such discussion would have been
Too embarrassing for me to sit
With, coz of how they would
Have spread the news.

Monday came, and I found my way
To a court so as to get the affidavit.

That was the first time I knew there
Was a Magistrate Court close to my
PPA (the Ministry of Justice), because
I previously didn't even know where
Any court in Enugu was.

Apart from the High Court I saw
That was along WAEC road abi
WAEC office.

I couldn't even introduce myself as a
Corper-lawyer posted to the Ministry
Of Justice, all I said was *"I'm a corper,
And I just came out of camp."*

Did I even just come out of camp?

I'd already been out of camp for more
Than a month, and exposed enough
To know that I wasn't supposed to
Allow myself to be scammed.

And did I even know how to draft
An Affidavit???

Law School was just for me to
Read and pass exams and get
Out of the place.

After more than half of the day gone,
(Arriving there eight on the dot and
Not leaving till past four), I finally got
The affidavit drafted by one of the
Paralegal staff.

Then proceeded to another Police
Station to make the report.

I didn't want to go back to the place
Where I was told to bring one thousand
Naira to get my complaints processed.

I felt since I now have an Affidavit,
The Police report would be free.

This female police officer listened to
Me and even took me to the SSO's

Office so I narrate everything again.

SSO now said if I want them to take
The matter up, I should bring ten kay,
That they'll prosecute the matter to
The end and ensure he is sent to jail.

That I lost twenty-five thousand naira to
Samuel Tuesday in a swoop of two days
Wasn't sad + bad enough for me.

That I spent another one kay and three
Kay respectively for the Court affidavit
And Police extract didn't even help
Salvage the situation or recover the
Money.

[Yes, when I couldn't pay the ten kay
The SSO was asking for, I had to settle
For three kay – which was the price for
A police extract at that station.]

I snapped the Affidavit and Police
Extract, sent it to Leo and he said
I should take it to the nearest UBA

Bank for further action.

After spending more than six hours
On a queue and everything till it got
To my turn, the bank people there
Now said they don't handle things
Like this, that I should take it to
There regional office at Trans Ekulu.

Another travelling and journey again.

I got to that place, the man I was
Referred to said *"do you have any
Lesson to bring out of this?"*

I said *"Yes, that I shouldn't trust
Online people again."*

He looked at me with that kain
Look and said *"No. The lesson is
That you shouldn't be greedy.
You were greedy!"*

Upon the yabbing and Ted Talk,
Nothing still came out.

All he said was that he had sent
The message up, but that they
Have no authority to block the
Account.

Because it's between two banks,
My UBA and the scammer's GTB,
And I'll have to send message to
GTB just as I've done here.

Hmmm! Another long journey.

The more I thought about these things,
The more the pains just wouldn't go
Away: as I was unable to come to terms
With how I could allow myself fall for
The simplest of all scams.

WhatsApp scamming!

I was ashamed of myself: barely spoke
To anyone about it, coz no one would
Understand how I could be that #?*#!

When I engaged in Double Cash few

Weeks later, it showed how desperate
I was to get my money back.

For an investment of seven thousand
Five, I could only gain five thousand
Naira.

Then I was duped again. This
Time around, on Facebook!

A ten thousand naira that I got from
My allawee the following month got
Hooked in a facebook scamming page
Known as Pillars Ng site.

Whoever was holding my calabash in
The village must have been laughing
Hard at a gullible idiot like myself.

In all, I lost over forty thousand
Naira.

For someone who wasn't used to
Getting/making money and just
Getting swindled for the first in

An attempt to getting money for
Accommodation, forty thousand
Naira was a huge loss for me.

Then I got introduced to betting
Later that same July, prior to the
Start of the 2018 FIFA World Cup
In Russia.

It's fun and entertaining.

That's all I can say as I see red
All over my stake analysis.

The struggle to win is real, but
The struggle to avoid a defeat
Is very painful.

One moment, you're excited about
How your bet has entered, the next
Second, you are finding it difficult
To understand how Barca can't
Score just one more goal.

I started with Bet9ja, making use
Of just hundred naira to bet during
The country matches.

Only for me to realize that I had
Put in more than five thousand
Naira, without getting anything
In return.

Out of frustration, I left them
And started using Sporty Bet:
In the hope that things would
Be get better.

I was happy for a while…until
My bet started cutting again.

Without even having the privilege
Or opportunity of withdrawing any
Money!

And this time, it even became more
Painful in that I started using them
During the Women's World Cup and
Africa Nations Cup 2019.

Then I told myself to wait until the
Start of 2019/2020 season, when I
Was believing I'll be able to make
Good money from the matches
That'll flood in.

From what I'd been winning, I had
Been able to raise six kay prior to
Man City's opening match in the
2019/2020 English Premier league
Match against WestHam.

Only for everything to cut in that match!

Coz I went to put under four point five,
When it was eighty minutes and scores
Was still three zero.

Man City scored two more
Goals in front of me.

It was then I learnt never to place
Under-goals in Man City's match.

In December twenty-nineteen when the

Season was getting to its half way line,
I had raised another money on Sporty
Bet through roll over.

This time, nine kay.

Only for stupid Ajax to lose one zero at
Home – in a champions league match
Against Valencia that I placed over
Two point five for them.

Ajax was a free-scoring side, it was
A must-win match for Ajax if they
Wanted to qualify for knock out
Rounds, so I expected nothing
Less than end to end goals.

Ajax had other plans in mind.

Now, after using consistency and
Perseverance to raise another three
Kay, I went to fling the money away
By putting over two point five in the
Tottenham-Liverpool match.

That particular match ehn, straight
Win and over two point five had the
Same one point seven five odds.

Liverpool was going on a winning
Run + clean sheet, and I wasn't sure
If Mourinho's Tottenham would try
To win by scoring goals too.

Liverpool won by just one goal.

The issues of betting started wearying
Me as we were getting into 2020, coz
It was now going to two years without
Cashing out.

Coz of one odd or the other gone wrong.

Even if I stake that all players will wear
Jersey into the field, one useless player
Will still enter the field without cloth.

And even if I stake that all players will
Wear boot to the field, someone will
Still jog in with slippers!

I don't know how to say it, but the
Pressure to make it in life isn't the
Way we thought it would be.

Many money problems everywhere!

Anything you want to do or get
In this life, you need money.

Job: Money. Love: Money. House:
Money. Sex: Money. Flex: Money.
Peace: Money. Death: Money!

Azin, even death is not free: to die
Gan, they'll still have to look for
Money to buy your coffin and
Dig your grave to bury you.

Like, I just don't get it again.

I have always learnt that we are
Not supposed to speak about our
Problems or predicaments, coz no
One gives a fuck about how we
Feel.

There is a sense of belief that everyone
Is only viewing us from afar - to be sure
We are not better off than them.

Or to check if hand of life
Haf finally hit us.

And this alone doesn't even
Want to make me relate with
Anyone publicly, for fear of
Show off.

Like, how on earth can I make it
In this life if everything I do will
Always cut like my bet or will
Shutdown like the pandemic?

And I know I'm not alone on this:
Many who try to engage in one
Form of financial investment or
The other have ended up saying
"Oh-my-gawd!" on some pretty
Annoying occasions.

It's either NNU becomes UNN,

BITCOIN beats their coins, their
LOOM ends up in DOOM, or the
Federal Government is placing
A ban on the Crypto world.

That's after CRYpto has made
You CRY sha.

I don't even seem to know what to
Make of the working career of the
Average African child anymore.

At a little age, it feels like the ones
Living before us have the absolute
Blueprint for life.

They tell you where to go, what to do,
Clothes to wear, who to meet, books
To read, and that you should focus on
Your studies.

Then we grow up only to find out
That they were only talking about
Their rules, their morals, and their
Religion.

Something that (arguably) makes no
Sense, and something that doesn't
Bring money to one's account.

The real money, which is the most
Important instrument to our survival,
They don't teach us to learn it or help
You to earn it.

Primary school, secondary school,
Tertiary, NYSC, and after then, what
Next? Does the job actually come?

Those that get the jobs and money,
Definitely, they must have two heads.

Or maybe three, or even four sef!

It feels like they are serving a different
God, or they are using a different jazz
I'm yet to be aware of.

Or they are even selling their kidney
To make ends meet, or using other
Parts of their body to keep alerts

Rolling in.

But, does going to school directly
Amount to getting a job?

If that were to be the case, why
Are we having so high a rate of
Unemployment?

And who are those actually
Getting the job?

From Lagos to Abuja, Enugu to Calabar,
And Kano to Sokoto, what everyone is
Looking for is a money to spend, means
To stay alive, and a hope to hang on to.

And whether you go to school or
Not, the struggle to succeed hits
Everyone deep and hard.

And at this point in time, I'm now
Asking myself what I am to do with
The ten percent principle, amongst
All the other principles that has

Been given to me.

"Give, and it shall be given unto you."

I give, but I don't get anything in return;
Instead, I hear people talk about how
"Helpers of destiny" have been giving
Them material and financial favors.

Without asking!

Even jobs!

How are these things happening???

I wonder…if I'm to save ten percent
Of my income, and give ten percent
Of my income to the church as tithe,
Why the fuck am I still poor?

Shey me sef nobi descendant of
Abraham ni?

Abi which kain sapa be dis one??

For me, right from time, I've been
Wondering how I'll get a job: coz
My kind of person doesn't show
Up as one who is created for a HR
Lifestyle, or office responsibilities.

Give me a job and tell me to work
From home, and I'm going to do
The job perfectly for you.

But not coming to the office and
Be doing nothing, just snapping
Picture with fine furniture and
Going to the lounge on the Island
To snap another so as to post on
Social media.

I do think I'm the only one who
Thinks like this (of not fancying
The office job thingy), but I know
A lot more are beleaguered by
This thought as well.

That is, the struggle to get a job,
Earn a living, and make it in life.

Sometimes, it gets worse when I start
Thinking *"omoooo, at 25, I'm still living*
In my father's house; at thirty, I've still
Not gotten a job; at 42, I've not yet
Built my own house!"

These things are killing to think of.

For a fact and truth, we need money to
Live/exist. And as much as the Christian
Faith or religious society want to place
God as the author and the finisher of
Our faith, or the provider of all things,
It doesn't feel like that is the case.

It seems as though that dude isn't
Authoring any fucking thing, that
He's just finishing the remaining
Faith we have.

And leaving us to our fate.

So, what to do?

I do absolutely nothing!

And right there, I was looking at how
Close-to-miserable my life had become,
Coz I concluded I could no longer convert
Anything I'm doing into something that
Can pay my bills.

Even if I want to say *"I love you"*,
Can she take it to the bank and
Cash out???

Expressions:
Dearest Suicide

Part 17: Men Have Feelings Too

It's page 379 and I still haven't
Killed myself huh?

You should be curious enough to
Know why, just as I am anxious
Enough to tell you.

The problem is that only few people
Talk about these things in this way
And manner.

Only few people.

And I don't just mean the absence
Of jobs, the loss of betting tickets,
The complex issues with romantic
Relationships, or the coronavirus
Situation as a whole.

You see, men are the ones who make
Suicidal decisions more than women,
And that is because men don't talk
About their suicidal thoughts when
They go through their tough stuffs.

Why???

Because men are societally wired to
Keep quiet on their problems and
Handle their crisis quietly and
Silently.

Without anyone knowing what's
Going on.

You know, "depression" and "suicide"
Contravenes the qualities of resilience,
Strongness, firmness, boldness, and
The "be a man" ness that has long been
Fused into our social construction

Into our masculine identity.

Such that, to admit our suicidal thoughts
Or contemplate on certain suicidal actions
Is to admit to our weakness and be seen as
Weaklings and a failure to the manliness.

Obviously, this is having some tragic
Repercussions in the lives of so many

Young and growing male child, and
Even the middle aged and aged men.

To put things in clearer perspective,
Suicide and attempted suicide is a
Very difficult subject to discuss
Amongst male folks.

Men rarely talk openly about their
Issues of depression or reveal the
Suicidal thoughts that go on in their
Head.

Without being gender biased and all,
One thing we always fail to accept is
That, unlike whatsoever we want to
Think of concerning female depression,
Male depression is as strong as, and
Even stronger than what we see.

We always suffer in silence. We always
Do. And we always wish we can also
Have someone look out for us and
Seek out ways to take care of our
Needs.

No matter the needs - even if we are
The ones being silly, annoying, childish
And not being "man" enough.

But we rarely ever have anyone to talk
To, stay with, understand us, or help us
Take away the pains we go through or
Feel.

Pains we can't talk about or share with
Anyone, because we are supposed to
Bone things, man up, and act like the
Tough guy that the babe expects us
To be.

That the society expects us to be.

And because of the poor mental health
Awareness that arises based on the
Sort of things we do go through, we
Are more likely to suffer from sadness,
Depression, and other forms of suicidal
Symptoms.

Without even knowing!

Or slightly knowing but not willing
To admit and acknowledge, either
By the men themselves or by the
Female fold.

Many words to say, but a times, mere
Words aren't enough to express what
Men go through when they experience
Heart breaks, failures, setbacks, and
Defeats.

We all go through various degrees
Of pains that'll cause us to break
Down, and sometimes cause us
To cry.

It's psychological. It's emotional.
It's depressing. And sometimes,
It's suicidal.

The feeling (however) that men should
Be derided for showing up emotions is
A prime example of why so many men
Don't feel confident in themselves.

And are always scared to open up
When they go through excruciating
Stuff.

Do you know that the biggest
Killer in men under forty is
Suicide???

And that this suicide is the after
Effect of an excruciating pain
Left unchecked???

And that's because we want men
To ACT UP!
And
MAN UP!

I have had a lot of lonely times with
Mad depressing thoughts, where the
Demons against me were hard and
Difficult to overcome.

Here's what I mean.

A girl once asked me *"how are you?"*

And I knew just what answer would
Be best for her question.

I mean, just say *"I'm fine"* and add
A smile that speaks of more lies
Than any atom of truth.

Game tweaked. Problem solved!

But why speak the truth when it
Isn't going to bring the required
Love that you're looking for?

The needed emotional drug to
Kill off the emotional pain you
Feel in the inside of you.

So I choose to lie. To pretend. To
Just say something that makes the
Talk end so quickly and make her
Leave my space swiftly.

It's not the case that I pretend to
Anyone about the state of my life,
Health, or feelings, or that I wear

A face mask of smiles to cover up
The deep hurts I feel inside.

However, there's a trick that always
Comes with me feeling this way; and
That one trick, apart from the silent
Treatments and withdrawal I give
Those around me…

…is that I write.

I mentioned it before. My Expressions.
Pouring out my mind in different series
And colors of words that expresses just
How I feel at any given point in time.

I write these things so as to make myself
Feel fine and not do any of the terrible
Things I always think of doing each time
I feel this way.

Feeling moody. Feeling down. Feeling
Unhappy. Feeling rejected. Feeling
Defeated. Feeling Depressed. Feeling
Suicidal. Feeling dead.

Feeling! Feeling!! Feeling!!!

I actually mean everything I say, and
Sometimes, I actually wish someone
Can understand the way I deeply feel
And come straight forward to help me.

Without me having to ask.

Especially my girlfriends – both the
Ones I deeply fall in love with, and
The ones who deeply fall in love
With me.

But the problem with this sort of trick
Is that, the moment someone tries to
Figure it out and begin to ask questions,
I find myself not having the desire to say
Anything again.

I lose the feeling to speak.

I just fall back into my problems and seek
A successful courage to say *"I'm fine"*, and
Even ask the person *"how have you been?"*

And that's even if I'm in
Good-talking-terms
With the person.

Or momentarily lock up: if the person asking
Has also distanced herself (it's mostly the girls
That do the asking and distancing) from me,
Leaving me to find a way to take care of my
Thoughts.

But deep down within me,
I know I'm not fine.

And deep down within me also, I know
That whatever I say to the person isn't
Going to make the person understand
Me or bring out the solutions I need to
Cure me of my problems.

Apart from a silly *"ehya, sorry."*

So why talk??

But I still talk all the same. To some
People. Even though they'll still have

One sort of thing to say 'against' me,
Or to question why I say what I say.

E.g: When I say I like sex, when I
Post naked girls on my WhatsApp
Status, or when I say I love to
Masturbate.

Maybe I should have man-ed up
Each time and pretended nothing
Was happening to me.

Maybe I should have written only
The good stuff about myself to the
Public.

But because of the fear of how I'll
Be seen or if my story would even
Be accepted, I try to hide and keep
My pains to myself.

In the belief that no one needs
To hear my story and any of the
Bad stuff running through my
Head.

Mtscheew! Nun-sense!

That's why I love the non African
Men and how they express their
Pains or stories.

They cry!!!

And that's the more reason why we
Need to empathize with men when
We find them in notable pains…

…like the inexplicable howlers of Karius
And the emotional wreckage he suffered
In Liverpool's Champions League final loss
Against Real Madrid in twenty-eighteen.

Those who watched that football
Match saw how broken-down and
Tearful he was at full time.

It was even Mohammed Salah's shoulder
Injury against Sergio Ramos that brought
The first tears to the team, but Karius'
Led to the team losing 3-1 to Madrid.

Sebi it was 'ordinary own goal' that
Escobar did, and he was shockingly
Killed for it by fans of the Colombian
Football team at the 1994 FIFA World
Cup.

And I don't mean it merely literally.

These problems could as well be suicidal,
And Karius – for one - needed every ounce
Of courage, inner belief and personal drive
He could muster in order to come out of his
Brokenness.

Of course, that match marked the end of
His Liverpool career, in part, as he lost his
Starting shirt, and has been continuously
Sent out on loan ever since, from whence
Little or nothing is known or heard about
Him again.

He was only twenty-five as at the time
Of that horrific howler against Benzema
And Gareth Bale.

Lionel Messi suffered same fate when
He cried terribly bad at the end of the
Penalty shootout in Argentina's loss to
Chile at the 2016 Copa America Final.

It was his second consecutive final loss
To Chile in two years, having already
Lost to the same team at the 2015
Copa America final.

Also losing in a penalty shootout,
After a zero-zero draw at the end
Of extra time.

And it was his third straight final defeat
In three years – beginning in Brazil, in
Twenty-fourteen, when he lost to
Germany in the World Cup final.

Having already been taunted that he
Can't win a trophy for his country at
Senior level.

And watching how his eternal rival,
Cristiano Ronaldo, won the EURO

2016 with Portugal weeks earlier,
He couldn't bear the pain of three
Consecutive final defeats anymore.

He announced his Argentina retirement
Moments later in a by-the-way press
Interview.

Only to come out of retirement many
Months later, after receiving calls and
Trolls from fans for chickening out so
Easily when it mattered most.

Something (we all knew) Cristiano
Ronaldo would never do.

And till now, he still isn't 'considered'
The greatest player in Argentina; simple
Because he hasn't won an international
Competition (especially the World Cup),
With the senior Argentinian team.

[Edit: We are aware of the 2021
Miracle in Brazil huh? Let's leave
It like that for those who don't

Know.]

When I read the book "Loose that man
And let him go" by TD Jakes, I saw a lot
Of boy-ish natures in me.

I then realized how much I had suffered
As a young lad due to my father's actions.

He got me so scared that I couldn't freely
Approach him - or anyone for that matter –
Without thinking I'd be bashed, blamed,
Or accused for doing something wrongly
Or not doing something DILIGENTLY.

Fear and low self-esteem killed my
Confidence and destroyed my ability
To speak confidently about anything
That concerned me or my emotions.

Or how I felt about anything.

I began hating the pressures and
Responsibilities attached to being
Called a man, and I couldn't be a

Man for whatever reason so called.
Even if I desirably desired to be.

Because the girls would always
Call me a short little boy.

To the extent that, tears, anger,
Silence, pains, and withdrawal,
Became my primary means of
Expressing myself.

Even up until adulthood.

Anthony Bourdain, talented celebrity
Chef, adventurous globe trotter, author,
And journalist - with a successful show
On - CNN was found dead in his hotel
Room in France in the year 2018.

At the age of Sixty-One.

He committed suicide by hanging.

It's hard to understand how someone
So successful in his career would be so

Conflicted with feelings of hopelessness
And depression - even in the middle of
Shooting a show in France – that he'll
Decide to take his own life.

Less than three weeks to his birthday!

This is someone that President Obama,
While being the American President,
Sought out to shoot a show with him,
Because he was so impressed by his
Creativity + personality.

When I googled to check what could
Have led to his death, I found nothing:
News outlets reported that there was
No foul play or external violence in his
Death.

The rich, successful and famous guy
Just killed himself…. "for nothing!".

Like I said earlier on, men go through
Depressing situations, and always have
The tendency of trying to keep things

To themselves rather than reaching
Out and asking for help.

Thinking they can fix the problem
On their own.

And like I kinda pointed out, it's not
A thing of pride, it's just what most
Of us have been raised to become.

There's the story of a dad of two who
Posted *"sorry I wasn't good enough"*
On Facebook before killing himself.

He was unable to cope with living,
After watching his father agonizingly
Die from oesophageal cancer.

While still being a teenager, he also
Had to watch his mum suffer, as she
Was diagnosed with cancer, having
To be put on life support.

Before she eventually died.

These things had a negative effect on
His mental health, as he kept pushing
The problems away, trying to man up
And take on the responsibilities of his
Family.

However, he wasn't able to overcome
Them in the end.

In the hours before leaving, he sent
Wave emojis to the many friends he
Had on Facebook.

And then committed suicide in his flat.

Then a single dad, with just £4.61 left
In his bank account, took his life - after
Waiting for weeks for credit loan to
Clear his debt.

Phillip Herron, a thirty-four-year-old
Single dad, with three kids to cater
For, was sinking in a debt of close
To £20,000 when he decided to
End his life.

His final act as he sat in his car was
To upload a picture of himself crying
On social media.

Minutes later, he was found dead.

In his suicide note, he said his family
Would be better off if he wasn't there
Any more.

Things!

A US soldier, Stewart Hampton, opened
Up in a TV documentary about a belief
That almost cost him his life.

Like many men in their forties, Stewart
Had been brought up with the saying
"Man up" constantly ringing in his ears.

He grew up believing men talking about
Their problems was a sign of weakness,
And he never had the boldness to ever
Open up about his dark days.

He explained:

"I was brought up not to talk about my
Feelings. Instead, you'd have a drink to
Deal with things or you go out on the
Town with the lads and have a fight.

"That was my coping mechanism and
That's how I would deal with things."

He then reached his lowest point in
His life where he believed he couldn't
Take it anymore.

With a decision to end his life
On the cards.

Thankfully, he wasn't successful and it
Marked the turning point in his battle
With his mental health.

Gone was bottling up his emotions and
Anger. Instead, Stewart started talking
To both professional counsellors and his
Loved ones about his mental health, and

The emotional crisis that came with it.

Now, that's someone's story.

You know, there's a terminology I
Have come to understand about
Adulthood.

It's called MIDLIFE CRISIS.

It's a transition of identity and self-
Confidence that can occur in the
Middle-aged life of individuals.

That is, both men and women.

But men especially.

And it's associated with those between
The ages of forty to sixty-five years old.

The term was coined by Elliot Jacques
(Pronounced as Jacks) in nineteen-sixty-
Five.

And it is said to be a situation that may
Lead to feelings of intense depression,
High level of anxiety, a sort of remorseful
Disposition, and a desire to make drastic
Changes to one's life due to previous
Events.

Men in midlife crisis usually feel this
Sense of hopelessness – the feeling
Of being trapped in a life that is so
Draining and constraining.

When here, they feel this feeling of
Emptiness and inactivity, feeling a
Need to break out in search for a
Life that's not going to choke them.

A life that's not going to make
Them to cringe.

But not everyone experiences this
Theory of "midlife crisis", as some
People believe that such term is
Just a social construct fused into
Our mental reality.

Nonetheless, this crisis is most times
Caused by a combination of changes,
Challenges and disappointments that
Comes up in their life.

Like misfortune in work or career,
Relationship complications, marital
Problems, and changes that comes
With having grown up children.

The interesting thing about this stuff is
That while research says it goes from
Three to ten years in men, women
Only suffer this crisis for about
Two to five years.

You sef you can imagine!

One study also suggested that comedians
Have unusual psychological traits linked
To psychosis.

You know what is Psychosis, right?

A serious mental illness (such as

Schizophrenia) characterized by

Defective or lost contact with

Reality often with hallucinations

Or delusions.

Canadian Comedian, Tom Stade, revealed

How he was always using stand-up comedy

To keep his suicidal thoughts at bay, as he

Spoke out about his battle with depression,

With a desire to spread awareness about

Male mental health.

Like most successful comedians, he is

Surrounded by the ambience of laughter

While on stage; but life off-stage isn't

Always as funny as one would expect.

With the comedian admitting that

There were times he felt so low he

Couldn't even get out of bed.

He said:

"The perception is that comedians are

Funny, happy guys; but this business I'm

In can bring you up and down, and there
Are days I didn't want to wake up.

"One minute I'm way up, the next minute,
I'm way down. That happens a lot, and I
Just can't see any positives.

"As long as everything is going good, I'm
Fine. But it's not a normal job, and all it
Takes is one bad show, or one bad review
To knock me back."

As at the time of giving the statement,
Forty-eight-year-old Tom believed he
May have inherited his depressive
Tendencies from his dad, who suffered
From mental illness all his adult life.

He also blamed the tendency on
Men having to bottle up their
Feelings.

He continued speaking:

"Without comedy, I'd start thinking

About suicide.

"It's that big a help to me — the one thing
That keeps me sane. I've been doing it for
30 years, so to take it away from me would
Kill me, I have no doubt.

"My shows are a form of therapy — my
Psychiatrist is a room full of 300 people.

"Instead of holding something in, saying
It to strangers who relate to it is definitely
A relief.

"If things are going well, I seem to
Be OK, but there are months when
I worry — 'why am I not getting this
Job?'

"Once I feel like that, I don't know
How long it will last. Maybe a week,
Maybe three months."

He has never sought professional
Help and admits he uses alcohol

To self-medicate.

"I think that's how a lot of people think
They can handle it. I drink Jack Daniel's.
I know it's a temporary solution.

"I also do guided meditation for fifteen
Minutes a day, to remind myself I'm
Something more than this.

"It's a big help.
"I've never been to the doctor about
It, but if my wife ever said I needed
To, I would."

Nonetheless, he proposed that men
Should be able to feel they can ask
For help: the more men are honest
About their feelings, the easier it will
Get.

And apart from footballers and comedians,
Pastors aren't above the pain and struggles
Of the everyday people as it involves suicide.

The son of well-known Pastor and
Author of "Purpose Driven Life",
Pastor Rick Warren, tragically took
His life a couple of years ago.

Matthew Warren, the son of the Rick
Warren, committed suicide on the sixth
Of April two thousand and thirteen, at
The age of twenty-seven.

Speaking about his son's death, Rick
Warren said he had struggled from
Birth with mental illness, dark holes
Of depressions, and suicidal thoughts.

Often times telling his dad "Dad, I know
I'm going to heaven. Why can't I just die
And end this pain?"

Rick Warren marvelled at his son's
Courage to keep on moving for more
Than a decade, in spite of the relentless
Pain he was going through.

He was found dead at his home

From a self-inflicted gunshot
Wound.

In another story, Jarrid Wilson, a thirty
Year old Megachurch Pastor, who ran a
Christian mental health outreach and
Suicide group called 'Anthem of Hope',
Killed himself.

The advocacy group, which was founded
With his wife in two thousand and sixteen,
Was designed to help people struggling
With depression and suicidal thoughts.

And sought ways to end the stigma of
mental illness by connecting people to
Resources, including a twenty-four-hour
Crisis line.

In spite of these outstanding moves, the
Senior Pastor couldn't help himself when
He needed his own resources the most.

He chose to kill himself.

What was most surprising about
His death is that, he had spoken
Openly about his struggle with
Depression.

And hours before his death, he
Tweeted *"Loving Jesus doesn't
Always cure suicidal thoughts"*.

He died on September 9 twenty-nineteen,
A day before World Suicide Prevention Day,
Which he had also posted about on Twitter.

Leaving behind two little sons.

Similarly, Pastor Darrin Patrick, the teaching
Pastor of a megachurch in America – Seacoast
Church – died on May seven twenty-twenty in
A self-inflicted gunshot wound that was ruled
As suicide.

He was fifty years old.

We may never know what might have led
To his suicidal actions, but having looked

Into his life online, I had this to bring out
From the little things that happened to
Him.

Particularly in his Pastoral ministry.

On the thirteenth of April two thousand
And sixteen, the Board of 'The Journey'
(The church he founded), removed him
From his position as the Senior Pastor.

Reasons they gave included *"Pastoral
Misconduct"* and *"a historical pattern
Of sin"*.

The historical sins were listed as: *"lack
Of self-control, manipulation and lying,
Domineering, misuse of power, and
Refusal of personal accountability."*

The news of his removal was published
In different Christian Press in the United
States, and he was made to attend the
Church only as a member

For more than two years or thereabout.

He had the opportunity of speaking at a
Conference in Las Vegas in the year two
Thousand and seventeen, where he talked
About the lessons he learned from losing
His Church.

This was after he joined 'The Seacoast Church'
As a Pastor, with the leader of the said Church
Restoring him to pastoral ministry, permanently
Losing 'The Journey Church' he had founded in
The process.

Three years after, precisely on May
Seven twenty-twenty, he committed
Suicide.

Now, back to sports.

I've seen and read several mind boggling
Stories of great athletes and world super
Stars who have had one thing or the other
To do with depression.

From Michael Phelps' struggles with anxiety
And depression back in 2018, Rafael Nadal's
Battles with depressive pains in 2011, and
Serena Williams' postpartum emotions,
Famous athletes have oftentimes been
At their lowest ebb.

With the world so oblivious to what
They were passing through in those
Times.

One of such is the reality that came
Upon Atalanta's Josip Ilicic in the
Mid part of twenty-twenty.

After the end of the 2019/2020 Italian
Football season, dude travelled to his
Country home in Slovenia to give his
Wife a surprise visit.

Only to find her in bed being
Heavily quarantined by another
Man.

Fully spelt out, he caught her

Having sex with another man
In his home.

Surprise visit gone wrong huh?

Ilicic had been in fine form for his
Club all season, scoring 21 goals
In 34 matches, including five goals
In the UEFA Champions League.

To the extent that the 'little heart' goal
Celebration he would always do after
Scoring was a dedication to his wife
Whom he adored so much.

Maddening.

I remember when the news of the cheating
Broke out, Atalanta was to play PSG in the
Quarter finals of the rescheduled Champions
League match in the post-covid era.

Ilicic was so heartbroken, distraught, and
Depressed with his wife's situation that
He had to absent himself from the match

"For personal reasons."

With further reports saying he was
Considering quitting football as a
Whole!

Because he was losing his motivation.

This is someone who at thirty-two,
Was just beginning to enjoy the
Peak of his career, and still had
Some good years of football
Left in him.

What about the relationship
Between he and his wife in
Itself?

Ilicic and his wife had been together
Since two thousand and nine, when
They met, having two kids within
That period…up until when he
Me her in bed with another
Man.

And then there's Tiger Woods.

The name forever synonymous with golf
Still rings in my head as I remember the
Times he had to endure series of backlash
From the media, with major companies
Withdrawing sponsorship deals with him.

This happened after confessing in early
Twenty-ten - in a live broadcast aired
Around the world - that he cheated
On his wife, Elin Nordegren.

This is Tiger Woods, someone whom
Many considered as the world's best
Dad some years before the 'tragedy'.

Having undergone a 45-day therapy
Program that began in 2009, he held
A press conference where he openly
Apologized for his acts of adultery.

As it were.

In the aftermath of the announcement

However, his wife couldn't handle the
Disappointments that came with the
Shit, despite initially stating that she
Would stand by him.

She filed for divorce in August 2010,
Walking away with close to a hundred
Million dollars in divorce settlement.

Of course, this development hit Tiger
Terribly, as he couldn't focus on his
Golf career again.

By twenty-fifteen, Woods was already
Desiring to end his career, after a back-
To-back injury set back frustrated his
Playing time.

And that was after suffering a second
Relationship crisis with his new girlfriend
(Lindsey Vonn) whom he had been dating
Since twenty-thirteen.

People began talking about him, saying
Things, judging him and commenting on

What they believed wasn't right about
Him or on what he did wrong.

Making things all the more
Difficult for him to cope with.

He forced himself into hiatus for
More than a year, not playing golf
Anymore in the process.

Between twenty-sixteen and twenty-
Seventeen, he in another relationship
Once again.

This time, with stylist Kristin Smith,
Though rumoured, before finally
Announcing in November 2017
That he was dating Erica Herman.

Such hectic rollercoaster
Of relationship troubles!

In the process of all these, Tiger found
Himself going on a ten-year run without
Winning a major trophy in golf.

To the extent of even dropping off the
List of the world's top 1000 golfers at
Some point in twenty-eighteen.

This is someone who was once the
World's number one!

In an attempt to come back to
Playing, he had this to say about
All he had been going through:

"When healed, I look forward to getting
Back to a normal life, playing with my
Kids, competing in professional golf
And living without the pain I have
Been battling so long."

Thankfully, he was able to win his first
Major trophy in eleven years at the
Twenty-nineteen Masters.

Even being awarded the Presidential
Medal of Freedom by President Donald
Trump in the same year.

The story could have been something
Else for him you know? As we've read
Stories of those who couldn't handle
Their depression, and…you know?

Especially popular figures.

Then there is a Lionel Messi (again) too.

On August 25, 2020, Messi dropped
A bomb shell on the world when he
Announced that he was set to leave
Barca.

I think things had gone so bad for him at
The club – things he had been bottling up
For years – that he had to hand the club
A transfer request.

In a bid to walk away for good.

A decision that came in the aftermath
Of the humiliating 8-2 pummelling in
The hands of Bayern at the quarter
Final stage of the Champions league.

A trophy he has been so desperate
To win since twenty-fifteen when
He last won it.

This time around, Barca was pummelled,
Battered, trounced, whipped, butchered,
Spannered, drummed, trashed, humped,
Raped, and finally dumped!

Even Coutinho who was on loan from
Barca to Bayern joined in the raping
Of Barca.

It was a complete disaster!

And with the way the club kept falling
At the quarter final stage year in year
Out – first against Juventus in 2017,
Manolas' Roma in 2018 and then the
Liverpool horror at Anfield in 2019
(Corner taken quickly), Messi was
Getting fed up of the trend.

But with the capitulation by Bayern
In 2020, there was no hope that he

Was going to win the Champions
League with Barcelona ever gain.

Increasingly frustrated with what he
Believed was a lack of direction from
The club president, Bartomeu, Messi
Was mentally out the door and in
Search of a new club.

Something many were excited about.

Now, we all know Messi to be a reserved
Personality who shies away from public
Media and prefers to internalize his pains,
Unlike his rival, Cristiano Ronaldo who
Voices out his pains and frustrations
Glaringly and publicly.

When Messi becomes sad + frustrated,
He withdraws from the public and no
One hears from him again.

Like, how do these stars get to have their
Low times and we don't see it (the men
Especially) ought to be a very amazing

Subject, right?

This was the same thing he did in 2016
When he announced his international
Retirement, and no one heard from
Him again.

And he only reappeared for the national
Team after much pleadings behind the
Scenes.

However, in this case, Messi had become
Emotionally saddened by Barca's transfer
Antics and the way almost everyone around
Him kept being pushed out of the club.

First with the sale of Alves in 2016,
Neymar in 2017, and the failure to
Replace Xavi and Iniesta – his engine
Men - who left the club.

To the extent that these things were
Affecting the team's lack of Champions
League trophy, with Messi not even
Being on the podium for best player

Of the year in the year 2018.

The first time it was happening
Since 2007.

He was ranked 5th that year.

A whole Messi!

Then in twenty-twenty, Suarez was
Told he wasn't needed in Barca again,
And the thing ended what was left
Of his threshold for pain.

I mean Messi.

Thus, with the transfer request,
No one heard from Messi again.

Until after two weeks when he
Decided to break his silence in
An organized media interview.

And he had a lot to say coz he
Was ready to express himself.

"It was a very difficult year, I suffered
A lot in training, in games, and in the
Dressing room.

"Everything became very difficult
For me and there came a time
When I considered looking for
New ambitions.

"It did not come because of the Champions
League result against Bayern, no — I had
Been thinking about the decision for a
Long time.

"I always said I wanted to end here and I
Always said I wanted to stay here. That I
Wanted a winning project and to win titles
With the club, to continue expanding the
Legend of Barcelona.

"And the truth is that there has been no
Project or anything for a long time, they
Juggle and cover holes as things go by.

"I told the club, including the president,

That I wanted to go. I've been telling
Him that all year.

"I believed it was time to step aside,
That the time had come to seek new
Goals and new directions in my career.

"He told me all the time: 'We'll talk,
Not now', this and that, but nothing.

"The president did not give me a clue
At what he was really saying, he only
Said at the end of the season I could
Decide if I wanted to go or if I wanted
To stay.

"And in the end, he did not keep his word.

"Sending the transfer request was making
It official that I wanted to go and that I was
Free and the optional year, I was not going
To use it.

"It was not to make a mess, or to go
Against the club, but the way to make

It official because my decision had been
Made.

"If I don't send the transfer request,
It's like nothing happens.

"Now they cling to the fact that I did
Not say it before June 10, when it turns
Out that on June 10 we were competing
For La Liga in the middle of this awful
Coronavirus and this disease altered all
The season.

"The president then told me that the
Only way to leave was to pay the 700
Million euros clause, and that this is
Impossible.

"There was another way,
And it was to go to trial.

"I would never go to court against
Barca because it is the club that I
Love, which gave me everything
Since I arrived."

A lot of words there. Words that if he
Didn't say, no one would have ever had
An idea how sad he was concerning the
Kind of environment he was in.

Messi also opened up on the emotional
Conversation he had with his family when
The backlash from the media was hitting
Hard on him.

"When I communicated my wish to
Leave to my wife and children, it
Was a brutal drama.

"The whole family began crying.

"My sons, they grew up here and are
From here. They did not want to leave
Barcelona, nor did they want to change
Schools.

"Mateo is still little and he doesn't realize
What it means to go somewhere else and
Make your life a few years elsewhere.

"Thiago, he is older. He heard something
On TV and found out something and asked.

"I didn't want him to know anything
About being forced to leave, to have
To live in a new school, or make new
Friends.

"He cried to me and said 'let's not go.'

"I repeat, it was hard, really hard.

"My wife, with all the pain of her soul,
Supported and accompanied me.

"It was understandable. It happened
To me. It was very difficult to make a
Decision.

"But I did feel hurt by things that I heard
From people, from journalists questioning
My commitment to Barcelona and saying
Things that I think I didn't deserve.

"It has hurt me a lot that things are published

Against me, and above all, that false things
Are published, or that they came to think that
I could go to trial against Barca in order to
Benefit myself.

"There was nothing wrong with wanting
To leave. I needed it, the club needed it
And it was good for everyone.

"I wanted to go and it was entirely my
Right, because the contract said that
I could be released.

"And it is not, 'I'm leaving and that's it'.
I was leaving and it cost me a lot.

"I wanted to go because I thought about
Living my last years of football happily.

"Lately I have not found happiness
Within the club."

Hmmm......

One thing with mental health struggles

(And midlife crisis) is that it affects those
Who least expect to be affected by it.

Based on the sort of world status they
Possess.

If we think those who are up there have
Nothing to be sad or depressed about,
Then hear what someone like Luis Suarez
Had to say concerning how he was treated
By the same Barcelona.

"There were other ways to tell me that
They wanted to change things. The way
It was done and the feeling that they're
Kicking you out is what hurt the most.

"Those few days were very difficult. I
Cried because of everything I was going
Through because I wasn't in their plans
Again and had to be training alone, and
Returning home deeply sad."

Suarez was kicked out of a placed he
Loved so much and had to be training

233

Alone, just to stay in shape and stay
Fit.

Even though he couldn't even say he
Knew exactly where next he was going,
Or what the future had for him.

But for Messi, he couldn't leave. Coz
They frustrated his plans in a way he
Least expected.

After all said and done, he said was
Going to stay and try to do his best
For the club.

But we know Messi too well, and we
Know he wasn't happy with his new
Decision.

I still believe Messi was fed up and
Wanted to leave; but because he
Was unable to go to war with the
Club or convince his family in the
Opposite, he chose to continue
Living with his pain.

Because he is a "man", right?

There are other stories I could have loved
To pick, like the mental strength Ronaldo
Has had to go through over the years, in
His constant comparison with Messi.

And in having to win five Ballon d'or and
Five Champions League (including four
Ballon d'or in five years, and 3 consecutive
Champions League trophy).

Also winning two international trophies
For his country in the process.

When he was previously on just one
And Messi was in the spotlight for
Being the best player in the world
And winning four Ballon d'or in a
Row.

Or is it the mental torture Fernando Torress
Had to endure when he couldn't score a goal
For Chelsea in as many appearances + starts
He had for them when he arrived for a then

British record transfer from Liverpool.

Fifty million pounds. You remember huh?

Or the one Griezmann had to go
Through in his first season at
Barcelona.

Abi is it Hazard's poor run of form since
His arrival in Real Madrid from Chelsea?

These men/athletes/ super stars endure
A lot of thick and dark mental clouds that
Makes them easily prone to going through
The most devastating of depressing times
Or crisis.

That's because no one knows when they
Are truly frustrated, no one knows when
They are deeply in tears - especially when
They go many months without a starting
Role, or many weeks without scoring a goal.

Or when they are goal keepers, conceding
Miserable and Karius-like goals.

Now, of all the stories I've brought out
In this chapter, the one that comes so
Dear to me based on how close I am
To the person is that involving the life
Of Reverend Isaac Adeyemi.

Or Pastor Isaac Adeyemi – whichever
Name you know/address him as.

I call him 'my bad guy'.

In December twenty-fourteen, his Church
Announced through a number of national
Newspapers that they had suspended him
From his position as the District Overseer.

Indefinitely.

Sighting several concocted allegations, they
Rolled out his offences as: insubordination
To the General Overseer, forgery of G.O's
Signature to secure a sixty-five-million-naira
Loan, and purchasing of private properties
With the Church's funds.

Remember, concocted allegations.

Publishing a disclaimer in the newspapers,
The Church rendered Rev. Isaac Adeyemi
A persona non grata, and gave a warning
To its members never to associate with
Him ever again, for whatever reason.

But the story gets more interesting
When you get to know some things.

In the year two thousand and seven,
Reverend Adeyemi started a musical
Concert within the Ikorodu town of
Lagos called Embrace.

It was something similar to what Pastor
Paul Adefarasin of House on the Rock
Does with 'The Experiecne' at Tafawa
Balewa Square (TBS).

But unlike The Experience that holds
Every first Friday in December, this
One holds EVERY GOOD FRIDAY of
The year.

Easter Friday. Irrespective of what
Month it falls on.

Now, in the year twenty-ten, Embrace
Concert clashed with a programme of
The Church at National level, as it fell
On the same day.

The then General Overseer of the Church,
Gave the permission that both programs
Can hold concurrently.

Two years after (in 2012) there was yet
Another clash in programs; and this time
Around, there was 'a new Pharaoh who
Didn't know about Joseph'.

This new G.O instructed that Embrace
Be cancelled, and that all members of
The District report for the National
Program.

Something that didn't go down well
With the organizers of the concert
(For obvious reasons, as millions of

Naira had already been spent in).

The G.O even strategically ensured Isaac
Adeyemi was given a segment to anchor
During the said national program, as a
Perceived ploy to test and see if he'll
Come or not.

A trap. A very good trap.

He was then queried for allowing 'Embrace'
To hold, despite the warnings of Daddy G.O,
And charged to the disciplinary committee
Of the church for sanctioning.

Meanwhile, he actually attended the
National program and did the task
Given to him there.

But because one of the Guest Ministers
Of the program, whom had first been
Contacted by organizers of Embrace,
Left the National Program (after her
Ministration) with Isaac Adeyemi
To attend Embrace, the thing

Shock dem.

Further allegations were later raised
Against Rev. Isaac Adeyemi, including
Disrespecting the G.O by talking to the
G.O with his hands in his pockets, and
That he must apologize.

My bad guy didn't.

Behind the scenes twist: Isaac Adeyemi
Was one of the contestants/nominees
For the office of General Overseer of
The Church, but ranked sixth in the poll.

[Yes, the Church conducts election
Every five years to appoint a new
General Overseer.]

And after Daddy G.O rightfully won,
He took a step further by calling out
Isaac Adeyemi and other "boys" of
The former G.O, that his eyes will
Be on them throughout his tenure.

So, it was already a….shey you get?

One thing led to another during the
Disciplinary Committee meetings,
And he was suspended indefinitely
By the Church.

With a plan to replace him with a new
Reverend: a Reverend whom Adeyemi
Once helped when that one also had
Issues with the same G.O and was
Removed from board of directors.

Of course, this was met with opposition
By Adeyemi's loyalists in his local church,
And before we could say jack, the name
Of the Church changed from Foursquare
Gospel Church to Embrace International
Assembly.

Bringing about an immediate
Division within the district.
For some beautiful reasons, a larger percentage
Of the Church weren't able to understand why
The General Overseer would decide to sack the

District Overseer, and indefinitely suspend him
From even being a member of the Church.

Just! Like! That!

While there were others as well who,
Irrespective of whatever must have
Been happening, didn't buy the idea
Of now being called a new church.

Well, Isaac Adeyemi announced to his own
Members that the church was no longer a
Foursquare church, because no one can
Suspend him from carrying out God's
Work.

That whoever wanted to go to Foursquare
Was free to walk out the door, and whoever
Wanted to stay with Embrace was welcome.

Within weeks of that decision, MOPOL
From Zone 2 Onikan, and some soldiers
Went to lockdown the 'new church'.

On the orders of the General Overseer.

You go fear action film na.

Omoo, members of the new church
Used pure water and what they could
Lay their hands on to chase away the
National officers who wanted to come
And take over the church.

I guess those ones were better prepared,
As they had their own soldiers too, and
Those ones were of higher ranks than
The ones National organized.

Well, the game switched, and the son
Of the suspended Pastor was arrested
In the home of the Pastor, and made to
Sleep in the police cell for several days.

Because they couldn't find
Isaac Adeyemi to arrest.

And they even took the matter to Court.

That is, National.

Things became utterly messy.

At a stage, the wife of Pastor Adeyemi
Had to go to the General Overseer to
Kneel and beg, crying and pleading for
Things to be resolved.

But all fell on deaf ears.
E kon be like sey Daddy G.O
No get spirit of forgiveness.

I can vividly remember in the year 2016
When I was the Zonal Youth President
Of my zone and had to be attending
District Youth Executive meetings.

The then District Youth Minister pissed
Me off with the way he was going about
Slandering the image of Isaac Adeyemi
On social media.

I mean, this is a man whose drama ministry
Was supported in every possible way by the
Then District Overseer, when no one was
Ready to support his project.

So, I wondered why he was insulting the
Embattled Pastor at every District Youth
Executive Meeting we had, to the extent
Of saying *"we will take back our church
From the thieves!"*

I was just twenty-three years old at the
Time, recovering from the depression I
Suffered with the extra year I had, so I
Couldn't understand why the Church
Building could become more important
Than the life of the Pastor they were
So kin on wrecking.

A church building the church at the
National level had no part of when it
Was still struggling to grow into what
They were now eyeing.

You know, we can never know the true,
Complete or exact story within the plot
As to why the Church (or should I say
The General Overseer) was hell bent
On 'destroying the life' of Adeyemi.

Reason being that many interest groups
Already have different versions to this
Story.

But one thing that became clear to me was
The reality that the leadership of the Church
Through the General Overseer, was hell bent
On ridiculing Isaac Adeyemi through a political
Vendetta, and taking away what he had spent
His hard earned life working and toiling on.

His spiritual ministry and his passion
For the gospel.

And for the Church's building to have a
Change of name from what it used to be
To what it now is, and even taking the
Pastor they've indefinitely suspended
To court, it sure signaled that a lot had
Broken down between both parties.

Irrevocably. Irretrievably. Beyond repairs.

Perhaps, forever, as the matter is
Still in Court, after being struck

Out on a number of occasions for
Lack of Jurisdiction.

Arguments can even be made on how
Wrong it is for Pastor Adeyemi to have
Changed the name of the church, rather
Than *"Let God fight your battles for you."*

But like I've said, people will only
Rant when they're not the ones
Wearing the pant.

It's not easy to make decisions, especially
After you have been disgraced, embarrassed
And humiliated by your own church, with your
Face slanderously printed in newspapers with
False and grave accusations.

Truth be told, Pastor Adeyemi even
Slipped into depression, unknown
To many.

Now, what would the church have gained if
The Pastor they so embarrassingly suspended
Decided to handle the pressure in a different

As the stories of the other Pastors shared in
Previous pages?

Well, one thing we know for sure is
That when Pastors are forced out of
Foursquare, they go on to become
Even greater and more successful.

As we proceed into the next chapter,
Have one thing at the back of your
Mind: **Men have feelings too!**

I'm not done talking about footballers
And their depressions though, as some
Actually died of it…

Expressions:

Dearest

SUICIDE

To be continued
December 12, 2022

Enjoying what you've been reading so far?

I bet you do!

Feel the heat! Feel the tension!

Feel the chaos! Feel the drama!

Dearest Suicide is a coming-of-age, controversial, and evergreen book that is a must-read for every teenager, youth, and adult of all ages, class, level, and grade. The book covers different areas and scope of the average adolescent and contemporary adult, from relationship, to sex, academics, religion, emotions, family life, work life, and breakups.

The author, PaGidi, is very detailed, precise refreshingly transparent, and direct, holding nothing back in this controversial yet moving story, which has changed the minds and perspectives of many since the May 12 edition was published. As you progress in each chapter, you will be conditioned to refer back to his disclaimer and warm advice time and time again.

There is vast amount of information from the book which can be applied to a number of human situations, not just suicide, and help people who have been hurting a long time, struggling with people who hurt them, or who are currently hurting. The timing of such a well-written-sensitive-yet-controversial subject could not be more perfect.

And if you haven't read the May 12 edition (When suicide becomes the healing you need), now is the perfect time to grab the book https://www.selar.co/dearestsuicide. *Just like Book 2 (Sometimes, DEATH becomes the only option) of the September 12 sequel, it contains never-before-seen experiences and personal stories based on contextual cases about the realities of suicide.*

ABOUT THE AUTHOR

PaGidi is all about giving humans the privilege and opportunity to speak their minds, express themselves, be listened to, and be understood.

Not just through written and spoken media, but also in person.

This he does with his straight-from-the-heart, non-conformist, direct and straight-cut blunt approach to controversial issues, using his unique writing style and relatable stories that comes with it as an avenue for people to shed off mental weights, emotional aches, and disturbing problems in ways that becomes a life-changing experience for them.

A self-professed non-practicing Christian, his writings are basically published on his social media accounts, and he has gradually become vocal on topics and issues not willingly discussed in the society.

Dearest Suicide is his second book.

If you would love to, you can follow PaGidi on:

Facebook: https://ww.facebook.com/pagidiexpressions

Instagram: https://www.instagram.com/_pagidi

Twitter: https://www.twitter.com/_PaGidi

Get the Paperback on Amazon: https://www.pagechap.me/PaGidi

And join the conversation.

You can also join **PaGidi Expressions official Whatsapp Group** by clicking:

https://bit.ly/3OH54Wi

To gain access to everything PaGidi writes about.

Including all of his Latest Expressions!

And keep up with his updates on Dearest Suicide.

It's time to begin those talks and conversations about suicide and stop the myths, stigmas, and African mentalities surrounding Suicide.

Dearest Suicide: Sometimes, DEATH becomes the only option, is A COMPLETE PACKAGE OF LOVE, HATE, TENSION AND NON-FICTION!

AND THERE'S STILL MORE!

Expressions:

Dearest Suicide

See you soon.

About the Book

In this long-anticipated and patiently awaited sequel, PaGidi continues the tale in his usual heart-grabbing and edge-of-your-seat conversational style by switching the rail from the narrative about his heroic pursuit of love in the midst of his academic woes.

Picking up right where Book 1 ended by giving us livid depths to circumstances leading to tragic deaths amongst teenagers, while baring it all in a villain role by revealing conversations about his girlfriend...as he begins his...second relationship?

About the Author

PaGidi is all about giving humans the privilege and opportunity to speak their minds, express themselves, be listened to, and be understood. Not just through written and spoken media, but also in person.

This he does with his straight-from-the-heart, non-conformist, direct and straight-cut blunt approach to controversial issues, using his unique writing style and relatable stories that comes with it as an avenue for people to shed off mental weights, emotional aches, and disturbing problems in ways that becomes a life-changing experience for them.

Dearest Suicide is his second book.